P9-DCC-384

Your Guide to Ecofriendly Decision-Making

practically
GREEN

Micaela Preston

Enjoy your green journey!
Micaela K. Preston

BETTERWAY BOOKS
Betterway Homes
Cincinnati, Ohio

Practically Green. Copyright © 2009 by Micaela Preston. Manufactured in China. All rights reserved. The patterns and drawings in the book are for personal use of reader. By permission of the author and publisher, they may be either hand-traced or photocopied to make single copies, but under no circumstances may they be resold or republished. It is permissible for the purchaser to make the projects contained herein and sell them at fairs, bazaars and craft shows. No other part of this book may be reproduced in any form or by any electronic or mechanical means including information storage and retrieval systems without permission in writing from the publisher, except by a reviewer, who may quote a brief passage in review. Published by North Light Books, an imprint of F+W Media, Inc., 4700 East Galbraith Road, Cincinnati, Ohio 45236. (800) 289-0963. First edition.

13 12 11 10 09 5 4 3 2 1

Distributed in Canada by Fraser Direct
100 Armstrong Avenue
Georgetown, ON, Canada L7G 5S4
Tel: (905) 877-4411

Distributed in the U.K. and Europe by David & Charles
Brunel House, Newton Abbot, Devon, TQ12 4PU, England
Tel: (+44) 1626 323200, Fax: (+44) 1626 323319
E-mail: postmaster@davidandcharles.co.uk

Distributed in Australia by Capricorn Link
P.O. Box 704, S. Windsor, NSW 2756 Australia
Tel: (02) 4577-3555

The pages of this book are printed on 60% post-consumer recycled paper.

Library of Congress Cataloging-in-Publication Data
Preston, Micaela.
  Practically green : your guide to ecofriendly decision-making / by Micaela Preston.
     p. cm.
  Includes bibliographical references and index.
  ISBN 978-1-60061-329-6 (pbk. : alk. paper)
  1. Home economics. 2. Sustainable living. 3. Green products. 4. Environmental protection. I. Title.
  TX145.P6835 2009
  333.72--dc22

                              2009016446

Editor: Julie Hollyday
Designer: Corrie Schaffeld & Rachael Smith
Production Coordinator: Greg Nock
Photographer: Ric Deliantoni
Photo Stylist: Lauren Emmerling

media
www.fwmedia.com

Dedication

To my boys—John, Drew and Liam.

Acknowledgments

I would like to thank Jessica Gordon, who championed this book from the very beginning, as well as my editor, Julie Hollyday, and my agent, Andrea Somberg, who expertly walked me through each new step.

Special thanks to my parents, Ivan and Robbie, who have cultivated my intellect and nurtured my creativity throughout my life.

And most of all, thanks to my husband, John, for encouraging me to follow my heart.

About the Author

Micaela Preston has a practical take on green living that she applies in her popular blog, Mindful Momma (www.mindfulmomma.com). Like many parents, Micaela cares deeply about the health of her family as well as the health of Earth. Yet she knows firsthand how hard it can be to keep on top of all the latest ecofriendly products and the most recent health scares... while still keeping the reins on the family budget.

Micaela has an MBA in marketing and enjoys applying her knowledge and understanding of consumer

Photo by Jeff Miller
www.jeffmillerphotography.com

behavior with her passion for safe and sustainable products. Her work as a brand manager in the food industry broadened her understanding of how food products get to our tables. She honed her passion for well-designed, high-quality products in the jewelry and home furnishings businesses and gained early insight into the importance of sustainable products as a buyer for a natural bath-and-body-care company.

Micaela lives in Minneapolis, Minnesota, with her husband and two boys. When she is not writing, she is busy whipping up a healthy meal or the eco craft du jour.

Table of Contents:

142

102

Introduction

Before I had kids, I wasn't exactly passionate about doing what was right for the environment. Sure, I recycled, but that was about the extent of my environmental activism. Back then, I was interested in eating well, but I had only myself to worry about. My salary was barely above minimum wage, so I shopped at resale stores for cheap, funky clothing. I had plenty of free time, and I made my own jewelry out of recycled necklaces and old buttons.

But now I have kids. And that changes everything.

Now I buy more stuff than I ever did when I was shopping just for myself, and I care about the impact those items have on the environment. Now that I'm cooking for two growing boys, I want to know more about the food I'm buying, both the benefits and the risks. Because of my kids, I am concerned about the amount of toxins in our lives. While my jewelry making has been put on the back burner, I am always searching for a creative outlet to fulfill my inner need to make things myself. And, most importantly, now that I have kids, I feel the need to make the world a better place for them to live.

That's where the concept of green living comes in. For me, green living means appreciating and protecting Earth so it is a healthier place for us all to live. It means being aware of my ecological footprint (the direct impact of my actions) on Earth. It means adopting a lifestyle based on preserving the environment and maintaining the health of my family through the choices I make and the products I buy.

I was inspired to write this book to help others navigate the complex maze of information about green living. Many of my friends say they are overwhelmed by all the choices they face in their busy lives. They care deeply about the environment, but they desperately want someone to pare down the information and make it easier to digest. That's what I've done in this book. My goal is not to bog you down with too many facts. Instead, I aim to give you enough information to make smart choices for the health of your family and the environment.

The Practically Green Approach

In my home, I practice my own version of green living on a daily basis. I like to call it the "practically green" approach. It's an approach that balances my interest in doing what's right for the planet and my family with the reality of constraints like time, money and whatever else is going on in my life. When I shop, I make the greenest choice I can, but I don't beat myself up every time I buy nonorganic food or cheap clothes at a chain store. My goal is to be mindful of my choices—not to be stressed.

I encourage you to try the practically green approach for yourself. Start small, perhaps by buying a few organic veggies or an energy-efficient light bulb for your home. As your personal care and cleaning products run out, replace them with ecofriendly versions. I'm not proposing that you head to the mall in the name of the environment, but rather that you use your purchasing power in an eco-minded way. Do what you can. If you find you can't afford something, or if it causes too much stress to go the greener route, stick with the conventional product—you can always choose the greener way next time. Just like fashion, do it with your own sense of style and your own creativity. Slowly but surely, living green will become a habit, and you'll forget you ever lived any other way.

Here's How the Book Works

You can dip into this book anywhere you like. If cleaning is at the top of your mind, jump right to Chapter 3 to learn how to clean your home the safe, ecofriendly way. Or skip ahead to Chapter 5 to find out how to green up your wardrobe. If you're the crafty type, get right to the DIY projects in the Do It Green section at the end of each chapter.

Throughout the book, my goal was to keep the information simple, the process creative and the outlook fun.

Creating a green and healthy home may seem like an overwhelming task at times, but if you use the facts and resources in this book and keep a "practically green" perspective, you can craft a sustainable lifestyle that works for you!

Chapter 1: Eating

100% Organic

Chapter 1: Eating
The Green and Healthy Kitchen

Many of my friends say they are desperate for a simpler way to navigate the grocery store. The sheer number of choices is overwhelming, even before considering the health and environmental impacts of the products they're about to buy. As they shop, a myriad of questions run through their minds. Questions like:

"If the label says 'natural' does that mean it's healthy?"

"What are the top organic foods I should buy if I have a limited budget?"

"Which eggs are better? Cage-free, organic, brown or the plain white kind?"

"Do fruit snacks really count as a serving of fruit?"

It's enough to make you drop your shopping cart and run for the hills to make a go at living off the grid. Barring that extreme solution, it helps to learn what you can before you go to the store because trying to make mindful choices in the middle of a busy store (or with an impatient toddler) is less than ideal.

If there's one thing I've learned in my quest to be a mindful grocery consumer, is that it's all about balance. I make constant trade-offs between what I know is healthiest and best for the environment and what I can afford, how busy I am and how strong my sweet tooth is that day. The 80/20 rule is often my guide as I try to ensure that the majority of the food I buy is healthy and ecofriendly while still leaving room for the occasional treat. I figure if 80 percent of my choices are healthy ones, the other 20 percent won't cause too much trouble. It's a practically green approach that works for me!

Hopefully, after reading this chapter you will feel more comfortable taking a stand as a green grocery shopper. The Buy It Green section will give you a better understanding of your food choices, whether you shop at a conventional grocery, a health food store, a food co-op or a farm stand. First, I'll show you the most common terms, labels and certifications you might find on product packaging. Next, I'll help you steer your cart safely through the store, pointing out the top tips for green and healthy shopping in each major department. I bet you'll feel like a green grocery superhero by the time you are through!

To mix a little fun into the sometimes tedious process of feeding your family, the Do It Green section has some creative earth-friendly recipes and healthy cooking ideas. I will explore the concept of the Earth-Balanced Meal—a healthy makeover of some dinnertime favorites. You will also find recipes for homemade grab-and-go snacks (minus the wasteful packaging of the store-bought variety) and delicious recipes and ideas for a healthy packed lunch.

11

Buy It Green

One of the most confusing aspects of being a green grocery shopper is the number of terms, labels and seals of approval used in the food industry, including quite a few that promote environmental, social and animal welfare causes. We hope these labels will help guide our choices, but they often merely add to the confusion. It pays to know the difference between terms that are meaningful and those that are simply greenwashing. Read on to learn the important buzzwords and relevant terms you need to know.

Organic
What Does It Mean?

Organic is a big-time buzzword in the world of food. But what exactly does it mean? In its most general sense, *organic* means that food is produced using environmentally friendly practices like soil and water conservation and the use of renewable resources. Organic farming methods, such as crop rotation, cover crops and the use of beneficial insects for pest control, maintain and enhance environmental harmony without the use of chemical fertilizers and pesticides. Organic animal production means the routine use of antibiotics and growth hormones is not allowed and also that the animal is fed organic feed, without any animal by-products.

The Organic Advantage

Organically grown food is clearly better for the environment, but it also has a benefit to the consumer, which is why so many of us buy it.

Organic food decreases exposure to pesticides. Pesticides have a number of negative consequences, including the following:

• Pesticide residues that are left behind on fruits and vegetables are impossible to completely wash off.

• Studies show a link between pesticide exposure and hormonal and neurological defects, even when the exposure is quite small.

• The risk to children is even higher because they consume two to four times more food per pound of body weight than adults.

Practically Green

Many stores now carry an organic store brand that is considerably cheaper than major brand named products. Whole Foods' 365 brand is one example, but your local grocery chain may have one, too. It's a smart way buy organic, as long as you're not stocking up on organic junk food.

Organic food offers nutritional benefits over conventional products, including the following:

- Organic produce has been shown to have significantly higher levels of cancer-fighting antioxidants than conventional produce.

- Researchers have shown that organic milk has higher levels of conjugated linoleic acids (CLAs), omega-3 fatty acids and antioxidants than nonorganic milk.

How Can I Afford It?

Organic food often comes at a premium price, sometimes up to 20 percent to 50 percent higher than similar conventional items. Because of the increased price, most of us have to limit our organic purchases to the most important items for our family. From a health perspective, you might want to choose the foods you or your kids eat the most.

Adventures in Green Living

Under the allure of the organic label, I let my son convince me to buy Organic Rainbow Rings. They sure looked a lot like Froot Loops, but somehow it seemed OK because they are organic. When I got home, I took to the Internet to find out if organic fruit loops are really any healthier than their mass-marketed counterparts. While munching away straight from the box, I found that my (I mean my son's) Rainbow Rings did indeed score better than Froot Loops on a number of measures. They had 40 percent less sugar, no hydrogenated oils, one gram more protein and 50 percent of the recommended dietary allowance for folic acid (versus 25 percent). Whew! But, honestly, do we really need organic fruit loops? In some ways, I think it is organic overkill.

14

Here are some top foods to consider.

- **Baby food.** A tiny baby is so much more vulnerable to environmental toxins than an adult. Why risk anything but organic?

- **Milk.** Milk is an important building block for strong, healthy bodies, and organic milk increases those benefits.

- **Meat.** Organic meat is free of pesticides, antibiotics and hormones you really don't want to be eating.

- **Carrots and potatoes.** Two of the most popular vegetables that are most likely to contain pesticides. That's not a good combination.

- **Peanut butter.** A staple food for many children, peanuts are also one of the most highly sprayed crops because they are prone to pests and mold.

- **Apples, peaches, strawberries and grapes.** These kid-friendly fruits are among the most likely fruits to be contaminated with pesticide residue, so buy organic as often as you can.

(Sourced from: "Dr. Greene's Organic Prescription;" Prevention "The Dirty Dozen;" The Daily Green "The Dirty Dozen: Top 12 Foods to Eat Organic.")

Shop Green

Look for the USDA Organic seal to ensure the product you are buying is certified organic. To use the seal, the following guidelines must be met:

- To claim the product is "100 percent organic", products must contain only organically produced ingredients, excluding water and salt.

- To claim the product is "organic", products must be made with at least 95 percent organically produced ingredients, excluding water and salt.

- To claim the product is "made with organic ingredients," the product must contain at least 70 percent organic ingredients, excluding water and salt. *(Note: the USDA Organic Seal may not be used in this case.)*

(Sourced from the US Department of Agriculture.)

Practically Green

Keep in mind that many small farms use organic practices even though they are not officially certified organic. Organic certification is expensive and time consuming, making it impractical for some farmers. Smart produce sellers will put up signs indicating their goods are "pesticide free" or "grown without chemicals." Don't be afraid to ask vendors about their farming practices—if they're selling at a farmers' market, they should be used to those types of questions.

Local
What Does It Mean?

Many people believe that buying local food is best for the environment, even if it is not certified organic. That's because the fewer "food miles" your food travels, the less energy it uses in the long run. Use your practically green sensibility to decide whether local or organic is the best choice for you.

Where Can I Find It?

- **Local farmers' markets.** This can be a fun family outing where the kids can meet the farmers and help choose the goods! In addition to local produce, you'll find local meats, artisan cheeses and delicious jams, preserves and other homemade foods.

- **Community Supported Agriculture farm share (CSA).** When you purchase a CSA, you are investing in a farm by buying a share of that farm's produce for the season. The amount of produce you receive varies by the farm, but if one share is too much for your family, split it with a neighbor. Get the whole family in on the task of figuring out what to do with the bag full of fresh veggies!

- **Community food co-ops.** Most food co-ops have ongoing relationships with local farmers and food purveyors. Next time you shop, make it a point to look for local foods.

- **Conventional grocery stores.** Many traditional groceries have picked up on the popularity of eating locally. Look for in-store signs showing product origins.

Natural
What Does It Mean?

The term *natural* is one of the most overused and misunderstood terms in the food industry. There is very little government regulation for the term, so it is used with abandon on all sorts of food products from fresh poultry to boxed cereal to frozen pizza. About the only thing *natural* really means is that it came from the earth, but not everything that comes from the earth is good for you. For example, chicken that has been pumped up with water, sodium and other additives can legally be labeled as natural, even though the excess salt isn't good for you. There are efforts to change practices like these, but for the time being, take this term with a grain of, um, salt.

Sustainable
What Does It Mean?

Sustainable agriculture is a way of raising food that is beneficial to the environment, humane to animals and respectful to farmers and farm workers. Food products do not have to be Certified Organic to be grown sustainably. For many farmers, sustainability is a way of life and is not necessarily a strict set of rules to follow. The challenge for the consumer is knowing what is truly sustainable because there are no federal standards other than Certified Organic. However, there are some reliable seals and certifications that embrace the principles of sustainability, such as Food Alliance, Demeter certified Biodynamic and Certified Humane. (See the Ecofriendly Food Certifications copy-and-clip guide on page 28 for more information about these and other seals of sustainability.)

Greenwashing
What Does It Mean?

Greenwashing is a term coined to describe the act of misleading consumers about the environmental benefits or practices of a product. With the popularity of the green movement, greenwashing has become quite common, especially in the food industry. Be on the lookout for:

- **vague claims.** Claims like "all natural" and "earth-friendly" are extremely vague and have no legal backing. Yet it is easy to believe products labeled with these terms might be better for you or the earth in some way.

- **irrelevant claims.** Stating that chicken has "no added hormones" is meaningless because by law poultry aren't allowed to be given hormones. That doesn't stop marketers from using the term on their packages, in hopes that you will pay a premium for it.

- **misleading packaging.** When you see a picture of a cow grazing on grass on your milk carton, do you assume the milk came from cows that actually grazed on grass? Think again. Just because there's a picture of it doesn't mean it actually happened.

Even Greener

Plant a garden and grow some of your own produce. If you don't have room for a full garden, try a few container plants for tomatoes, peppers or herbs. It's a great way to let your kids see firsthand where their food comes from. And what tastes better than a home-grown tomato?

Be a Green Grocery Superhero

There's really no need to be intimidated by all the product choices in the store. Instead, you can be confident you are making smart, informed decisions based on what you learn in this chapter. Think of yourself as a green grocery superhero—boldly buying what is best for the environment and for the health of your family. Don your cape and come along for the ride as we hit the aisles to find the most valuable green grocery tips for each department in the store. And don't worry, the green police won't arrest you for making a less than sustainable choice every once in a while.

Produce

Typically the first section you hit in the grocery store, the produce department is a great place to start buying green. For most people, a complete switch to only organic produce is out of budget, but fortunately, there are other ways to make sure your fruits and veggies are sustainable for the planet.

- **Organic.** Certified organic produce has a PLU code starting with the number 9 on the sticker. Use the Produce Safety Guide (see page 20) to avoid the most heavily contaminated fruits and vegetables. If cost is a concern, focus on what you eat the most—for some families that would be apples, for others, perhaps grapes.

- **Local.** Fewer "food miles" means less fuel was used to bring you your food. Smart stores have signs indicating locally sourced produce.

- **In season.** Don't make your veggies travel across the world for you. If you challenge yourself to stick to what's in season, your food miles will almost surely go down. Your food dollars probably will, too.

- **Fresh.** Whether you buy organic or conventional, from near or from afar, fresh produce is an important part of any diet, and it tastes great!

Dairy and Eggs

The dairy farm where contented cows graze in large, open fields is more likely a fairy tale than a reality. Factory farms with less than ideal environmental and animal welfare conditions are the norm today. Fortunately, more sustainable options do exist—you just need to understand the label. And choosing a more sustainably produced product has benefits both for your health and for the environment.

- **Organic.** Organic eggs and dairy products come from laying hens and cows that are fed only organic feeds and not given growth hormones or antibiotics. Cattle must graze on pasture during the growing season, and hens must be given access to the outdoors. Studies show health benefits as well: Organic milk has an increased level of omega-3 fatty acids and antioxidants over conventional milk, and organic eggs are high in omega-3 fatty acids.

- **rBGH-free.** Milk labeled rBGH-free is produced conventionally but without the synthetic growth hormones. Hormone-free milk typically costs a bit more than conventional but not as much as organic, making it a good compromise if you can't afford organic every time. Look for rBGH-free yogurt, cheese and ice cream as well.

Even Greener

Freeze fresh, seasonal fruits and vegetables to use during the long winter months. Diced fruits are perfect for smoothies, or you can puree fruit and save it in small containers for sauces or toppings. Blanch (boil briefly and then chill in ice water) and freeze vegetables to throw into a hearty soup or stew at any time of year.

Health Alert: rBGH

Recombinant bovine growth hormone (rBGH) is a synthetic growth hormone given to cows to increase their milk production. It is bad news for cows because it can lead to an udder infection called mastitis and the need for antibiotic treatment. If you're a nursing mom and have had the unfortunate luck to experience mastitis yourself, you'll know what that means. It's no fun for the cows either.

The side effects of rBGH on humans are subject to much debate. What is clear is that milk from cows treated with rBGH has high levels of insulin-like growth hormone (IGF-1). Some studies have linked elevated blood levels of IGF-1 to an increased risk of breast, colorectal and prostate cancers.

(a copy-and-clip guide)

Produce Safety Guide

Hardly anyone I know can afford to buy all organic produce all the time. The "practically green" approach to managing this dilemma is to focus on avoiding the most heavily contaminated produce. Take this list with you to the grocery as a reminder.

	Most Contaminated with Pesticides *(always buy organic)*	**Medium Pesticide Residue** *(try to buy organic)*	**Lowest Pesticide Residue** *(buy conventional with less concern)*
Fruits	Apple Cherries Grapes—imported Nectarine Peach Pear Strawberries	Banana Cantaloupe Cranberries Grapefruit Grapes—domestic Honeydew melon Orange Plum Raspberries Tangerine	Kiwi Mango Papaya Pineapple Watermelon
Vegetables	Bell pepper Carrot Celery Kale Lettuce	Collard greens Cauliflower Cucumber Green beans Pepper Potato Mushrooms Spinach Summer squash Winter squash	Asparagus Avocado Broccoli Cabbage Eggplant Onion Sweet corn Sweet peas Sweet potato Tomato

Sourced from: Environmental Working Group "Shopper's Guide to Pesticides," with data from the US Department of Agriculture and the US Food and Drug Administration.

- **Grass-fed.** Cows are given a steady diet of, you guessed it, grass. The milk they produce is higher in healthy fatty acids like CLAs, vitamins A and E and omega-3 fatty acids. The cows get plenty of fresh air and roaming time, unlike most conventional dairy cows.

- **Cage-free eggs.** Laying hens are not confined to cages and are given enough space to engage in natural behaviors. Look for the Certified Humane seal to ensure that eggs are from a cage-free environment.

- **Local or small dairy farms.** Supporting a local or small dairy farm often means you're buying into animal- and earth-friendly practices. If you're not sure of the farm's practices, ask.

Meat

Meat production can be a mystery. That's because most of us don't really want to know about where the meat we consume comes from. But it is important to understand the impacts meat production has on our planet and our health. For one, the meat industry is a notorious environmental polluter. The production of a single hamburger patty requires enough

fuel to drive twenty miles. There are also health concerns about residues from pesticides, antibiotics and hormones that can accumulate in the fatty tissues of animals and pass directly to those who eat the meat.

When shopping for meat, you will notice a slew of labels that identify the way the meat was produced. Be wary: Some of these labels indicate verifiable standards, while others are quite ambiguous claims with no legal meaning.

Practically Green

Choose the product you consume the most, whether it's milk, yogurt, cheese or eggs, and try to buy organic at least half the time. That way you're getting the benefits through the foods you eat the most.

- **Certified Organic.** This label is verifiable and identified by the USDA Organic seal. Animals are raised on 100 percent organic feed. No growth hormones, antibiotics or animal by-products are allowed. Animals must have access to the outdoors and freedom of movement.

- **Certified Humane.** This label is verifiable and identified by the Certified Humane seal or the American Humane Certified seal. Both groups ensure that animals live under humane conditions that allow for natural behaviors and provide adequate living space.

- **Free-range or pasture-raised.** No real standards or verification exist for this label. For poultry, the USDA states "Producers must demonstrate to the agency that the poultry has been allowed access to the outside." This does not mean, however, that the chickens actually did go outside.

Many "free-range" chickens are really cooped up in crowded pens for most, if not all, of their short, miserable lives.

- **Grass-fed.** The USDA has standards (diet must be 99 percent grass fed) but no certification for products carrying this label. Grass-fed cattle usually have higher levels of omega-3 fatty acids, vitamins A and E, CLAs (a good fat and potential cancer fighter) and lower levels of saturated fat. On the flip side, less fat can mean tougher meat, and some say the slightly "grassy" flavor is an acquired taste.

- **Natural.** A very ambiguous label, *natural* officially means only that the meat was minimally processed and does not contain any artificial ingredients, colors or preservatives. Look closely at the label for other info that might also say things like "antibiotic-free," "growth-hormone-free" or "100 percent vegetarian-fed." You really have to read carefully and ask questions when you see this label.

Shop Green

Don't be fooled into thinking brown eggs are healthier than white eggs. They're not. They're just brown. Some stores charge more because of a perceived health difference that simply doesn't exist.

Adventures in Green Living

I find meat one of the most challenging food products to buy. The ambiguity in labeling can be quite frustrating at times. Take this example: I was shopping for ground beef and picked up a brand that claimed to be naturally and humanely raised and handled. This claim spoke to the values that are important to me, so into the cart it went. At home I took a closer look. The package bore neither of the recognized or federally sanctioned certifications for humanely raised meat that were familiar to me. Instead, the package stated the meat was "humanely raised and handled as verified by affidavit." Maybe it was legitimate, but it was not verifiable by the average consumer. What's the solution? Unfortunately, there is no easy answer. Ask your grocer for answers and use your best judgment.

Eco-Alert:
Factory Farms

The majority of the meat we eat comes from concentrated animal feeding operations (CAFOs), also known as factory farms. You wouldn't want to discuss the details of a CAFO in polite company, but just know that concerns abound about these enormous livestock operations, including issues of animal welfare, public health and environmental impact. If you would rather not support factory farms, buy Certified Organic meat instead.

Even Greener

One of the most impactful things you can do for the environment is to eat less meat. Here's how to pull it off:

• **Go vegetarian once or twice a week.** Once you get the hang of making meatless meals, you might even do it more often.

• **Use less meat in your meals.** Flexitarians follow a semi-vegetarian diet allowing for occasional meat consumption. Try flexitarian recipes which use meat almost as a flavoring (think bacon) or a supplement to the meal instead of the main course.

23

Seafood

How do you view seafood? As a special treat, an important dietary staple or a potentially dangerous substance? The seafood industry has been plagued by conflicting messages about the health impacts of consuming seafood and about the negative environmental effects of large-scale seafood production. On the positive side, fish has been lauded as a source of heart-healthy omega-3 fatty acids. For that reason, the American Heart Association recommends you eat fish at least twice a week. On the flip side, concerns about the mercury content in some fish have people thinking twice about serving seafood for dinner.

Our love of seafood has some big-time environmental consequences as well. Overfishing has led to a risk of extinction of popular species and is unsustainable in the long run. Fish farming, the seafood industry's answer to the supply problem, is not a sustainable solution either.

Health Alert:
Mercury

Methylmercury, the type of mercury found in many fish, is a dangerous neurotoxin. Prolonged exposure to mercury can damage the brain and nervous system. However, the Environmental Protection Agency (EPA) says the health benefits of eating seafood override the potential negative effects, as long as we consume it at the recommended levels.

To help protect the health of your family, the Natural Resources Defense Council (NRDC) has a handy wallet guide about mercury contamination in fish (www.nrdc.org/health). Print it out and bring it with you the next time you shop for seafood.

Fortunately for seafood lovers, it is possible to find seafood from sustainable sources. Look for the Marine Stewardship Council logo to assure you the product is certified sustainable and use the Sustainable Seafood Guide on the following page, to help you make smart choices at the seafood counter.

Shop Green

For instant answers to all your seafood questions, use the FishPhone from the Blue Ocean Institute. FishPhone is a text-messaging service that puts sustainable seafood information at your fingertips. Just text 30644 with the message *FISH* and the name of the fish in question. You'll get answers and recommendations back in no time.

Sustainable Seafood Guide

Bring this handy copy-and-clip guide with you when you shop. It has great tips for buying the types of seafood most likely to make their way onto your dinner plate.

- **Salmon.** When you're buying salmon, keep two things in mind: wild-caught, not farmed, and Pacific, not Atlantic. Most Atlantic salmon comes from large-scale fish-farming operations, notorious for creating environmental pollution.

- **Whitefish** *(such as cod, halibut, flounder and sole).* Look for fish raised in the Pacific; avoid the Atlantic unless it's caught by a good, old-fashioned hook. When it comes to tilapia, US-farmed is preferred over imported due to heavy pollution.

- **Tuna.** Canned chunk light tuna (yellowfin and skipjack) is lower in mercury than albacore tuna, and the species are more abundant, making it the preferable choice.

- **Shrimp.** Shrimp that are wild-caught in the US or British Columbia are preferred, with US-farmed being a good alternative. Avoid imported shrimp because production methods cause pollution and habitat loss.

- **Shellfish.** Most other shellfish (clams, mussels and oysters) are OK, but when it comes to crab, steer clear of imported king.

- **Scallops.** Farmed bay scallops are preferred over sea scallops because they pose few environmental threats.

(Source: Monterey Bay Aquarium and Blue Ocean Institute)

(a copy-and-clip guide)

Beverages

Beverage marketers would have us believe we absolutely need to buy their products. And lots of them. The truth is, we don't need much more than good old tap water to meet our hydration needs. And just think of all the bottles we could keep out of the landfill if we eliminated single-serving beverages from our lives!

- **Bottled water.** Just skip it! The mountain of empty plastic bottles is terrible for the environment. Filtered tap water is just as good and practically free. Invest your money in a refillable water bottle instead.

- **Juice.** Beware the ubiquitous "juice drink" that is mostly sugar and maybe 3 percent juice. Instead, opt for 100 percent juice, purchased in large, recyclable containers instead of disposable juice boxes. Buy organic when you can.

- **Coffee and tea.** Our favorite morning ritual has some big-time environmental and social impacts. By purchasing Fair Trade Certified or Certified Organic, you are supporting a system that is fair to workers and better for the environment.

- **Soft drinks.** Even "natural" sodas contain plenty of sugar, so drink them as occasional treats.

- **Energy drinks.** Avoid these new-fangled drinks loaded with sugar and high doses of caffeine. If you need energy, try going for a jog or a brisk walk instead.

Adventures In Green Living

Early on, our day-care provider told us "juice is a trap that parents fall into." We didn't really get it at first, but as our baby developed into a demanding toddler we realized that it was oh, so true! Before I knew it I was keeping juice boxes stocked in the refrigerator and pulling them out for much more than just road trips. It took a while, but I did eventually get out of the "juice trap." My kids still enjoy juice, but I limit their servings—and juice boxes are a thing of the past!

The Rest of the Store

Once you've taken care of the essentials, you're still not in the clear. The interior of the grocery store is packed with aisle after aisle of boxed, bagged, canned, jarred, frozen and usually highly processed foods. Shop carefully to avoid excess packaging and unhealthy choices.

DO

- **Buy from the bulk bins**. Purchase foods from the bulk bins to limit wasteful packaging. (See Chapter 6 for more information on buying in bulk.)

- **Go for large containers.** As long as you have the space to store it, buy the largest container you can find. It's probably cheaper on a per-ounce basis, and you'll be saving an extra box or can from the landfill.

- **Support fair trade.** When you buy staples like sugar, rice, vanilla or chocolate (yes, that counts as a staple), look for the Fair Trade Certified seal. It ensures that laborers earn fair wages and working conditions are safe. Also look for packaged products such as cake mixes and even ice creams that contain fairtrade ingredients.

- **Buy food with short ingredient lists.** The longer the ingredient list, the more chemicals that are probably in it. If you can't pronounce it, you probably don't want to eat it.

DON'T

- **Fall for greenwashing.** It's especially prevalent in processed foods like chips, cereals and cookies. Remember, just because it's organic doesn't mean it's healthy.

- **Buy food in individual packages.** Think of all that waste! At least limit them to occasional purchases for road trips or parties.

- **Support GMOs.** There's much we don't know about genetically modified organisms (GMOs) and their effects on humans. They simply haven't been a part of our diets for long enough—it's best to steer clear if you can. There are currently no federal labeling requirements for GMOs, but some companies do opt to label products GMO-free.

Practically Green

Stick to the perimeter of the grocery store as much as you can. Only venture inside with a set list and a strong resolve!

27

(a copy-and-clip guide)

Ecofriendly Food Certifications

Name	What it means	Where to find it
USDA Organic	Conforms to all USDA Organic standards (see page 15 for details).	• Fruits and vegetables • Dairy and eggs • Meat and poultry • Packaged goods • Coffee and tea • Most grocery stores and food co-ops
Certified Naturally Grown	Farms follow USDA Organic standards but have sales of less than $5,000 per year and therefore do not qualify for the USDA Organic seal.	• Fruits and vegetables • Grocery stores and food co-ops • Farmers' markets and CSAs
Certified Humane	Products are produced with the welfare of the farm animal in mind. Sponsored by the American Society for the Prevention of Cruelty to Animals (ASPCA).	• Meat and poultry • Dairy and eggs • Grocery stores and food co-ops • Farmers' markets
American Humane® Certified	Guarantees that products are from animals raised and treated humanely.	• Meat and poultry • Dairy and eggs • Grocery stores and food co-ops
Food Alliance	Uses comprehensive standards and third-party inspections to evaluate entire farms, specific crops and food processors, packers, and distributors on sustainable agricultural and facility management practices.	• Fruits and vegetables • Dairy • Meat and poultry • Grocery stores and food co-ops • Farmers' markets

Take this guide with you to the grocery store to help decipher
the many certifications and seals of approval found on food products.

Name	What it means	Where to find it
Whole grain WHOLE GRAIN 8g or more per serving — EAT 48g OR MORE OF WHOLE GRAINS DAILY 100% WHOLE GRAIN 16g or more per serving — EAT 48g OR MORE OF WHOLE GRAINS DAILY Courtesy Oldways and the Whole grain Council. www.wholegraincouncil.org	Requires that the product contains at least eight grams of whole grain per serving. A 100 per-cent Whole Grain stamp requires that all the grain used is whole grain.	• Packaged foods like breads, cereals, crackers and pastas • Flours and baking mixes • Refrigerated and frozen entrees and snacks • Most grocery stores and food co-ops
Demeter Certified Biodynamic ® DEMETER CERTIFIED BIODYNAMIC®	A holistic approach to farming with very stringent environmental guidelines.	• Fruits and vegetables • Grocery stores and food co-ops • Farmers' markets and CSAs
Marine Stewardship Council MARINE STEWARDSHIP COUNCIL Licence Code 10108 © www.msc.org msc.org	The world's leading certification program for sustainable and well-managed fisheries.	• Seafood: fresh, frozen, chilled, canned or smoked • Most grocery stores and food co-ops
Dolphin safe	Ensures that tuna is caught by methods that do not harm dolphins and protect the marine ecosystem.	• Canned tuna (fresh tuna is harvested in a way that does not harm dolphins) • Most grocery stores and food co-ops
Fair Trade Certified	Guarantees that strict economic, social and environmental criteria were met in the production and trade of the product.	• Coffee and tea • Chocolate • Sugar and honey • Rice • Vanilla • Fresh fruit • Most grocery stores and food co-ops

Do It Green

Cooking and preparing food is one of the easiest ways to start living mindfully and sustainably. Sure, it may not happen every night, but do your best to slow down and enjoy the process of creating a delicious homemade meal for your family. Be thankful for the high-quality organic and local ingredients you buy and for the people who grow them. Appreciate the act of sitting down at the table with your loved ones. Then dig in and reap the benefits of your labors!

For all the recipes in this chapter, use organic and sustainably produced ingredients whenever possible.

The Earth-Balanced Meal

Just like we learn to take a balanced approach to healthy eating, we can take a balanced approach to eating with the environment in mind. Instead of an all-or-nothing green mandate, take the "earth-balanced" approach. The earth-balanced approach allows for a practical mix of earth-friendly, healthy and convenient ingredients: organic and conventional, local and imported, homemade and store-bought—you get the picture. If I make a homemade birthday cake using organic milk and cage-free eggs, I won't sweat the fact that I used conventional all-purpose flour. If I serve vegetarian meals a couple times a week, I'm not going to feel guilty about buying a steak for a special occasion. Try substituting an earth-friendly ingredient or two in your next meal.

Adventures in Green Living

In my attempts to make more earth-balanced meals, I've been actively trying to cut back the amount of meat I use. One of my strategies is to use only half a package of meat at a time. For example, if I'm making a stir-fry, I might use half a typical package of chicken breasts and make up the difference in veggies. The remaining meat goes in the freezer for another day.

Pizza Puffys

Next time you're about to grab a frozen pizza, try making Pizza Puffys instead. Kids just love this egg-based dish that is a cross between a pancake, an omelet and a pizza! It puffs up dramatically in the oven, and you can customize with whatever ingredients you or your children like. Much tastier than a frozen pizza, Pizza Puffys are homemade from healthy ingredients with no preservatives and can be the centerpiece of a meat-free or low-meat meal.

Ingredients

½ cup (114g) all-purpose, unbleached flour

2 eggs

½ cup (117ml) milk

2 T (28g) butter

Directions

Preheat oven to 400°F (205°C). Mix flour, eggs and milk together. Batter will be a bit lumpy. Melt butter in a 9" (23cm) pie dish. Pour in batter. Bake for 20 minutes or until light golden brown and puffy.

Serve immediately as is, or sprinkle with shredded cheese and other topping ingredients and pop it back in the oven for another 5 minutes.

Serves 4-6.

Try these fun varieties

Traditional Pizza Puffy

¼ cup (58ml) tomato sauce, spread on bottom of puffy

½ cup (114g) shredded mozzarella cheese

½ cup (114g) sliced pepperoni or salami (optional)

Veggie Pizza Puffy

½ cup (114g) chopped, cooked broccoli

½ cup (114g) cooked corn kernels

½ cup (114g) shredded Monterey Jack cheese

Mexican Pizza Puffy

¼ cup (58ml) salsa, spread on bottom of puffy

½ cup (114g) black beans

½ cup (114g) shredded cheddar cheese

Very Veggie Loaf

Instead of a boring old meat loaf, try this delicious and super-healthy veggie loaf. It is loaded with fresh vegetables, brown rice, nuts and cheese and can easily be customized with your favorite ingredients.

Ingredients

Cheesy Cashew Carrot Veggie Loaf

2 T (30ml) vegetable oil, plus oil for loaf pan

1 cup (228g) diced onion

1 large clove garlic, minced

2 cups (457g) grated carrot

2½ cups (571g) cooked brown rice

1 cup (228g) cottage cheese

2 cups (457g) shredded Monterey Jack cheese

1 cup (228g) chopped, toasted cashews

4 large eggs

1 tsp. (5g) cumin

½ tsp. (2g) salt

2 T (28g) chopped parsley

Directions

Preheat oven to 350°F (177°C). Coat a 9" × 5" (25cm × 13cm) loaf pan with oil or cooking spray.

Heat vegetable oil in a large frying pan over medium heat. Add onion and garlic and sauté until softened, about 3 to 5 minutes. Add grated carrot and sauté another 5 minutes. Let cool.

In a large mixing bowl, combine rice, cottage cheese, Monterey Jack cheese, cashews and eggs together. Stir in carrot mixture. Add cumin, salt and parsley and mix well.

Pack mixture into prepared loaf pan. Bake for about 60 minutes until firm to the touch and brown around the edges. Let cool for at least 15 minutes. Unmold and slice to serve.

Serves 4-6.

Variation: Broccoli Walnut Pesto Veggie Loaf

Use the same ingredients and directions as above, with the following changes:

Substitute 2 cups (457g) broccoli florets for grated carrot.

Substitute 1 cup (228g) toasted walnuts for cashews.

Substitute 2 T (28g) prepared pesto for chopped parsley.

Eliminate cumin.

33

Farmers' Market Fruit Crisp

Try your hand at a homemade fruit crisp that is much healthier than store-bought desserts loaded with ingredients you can't pronounce. Pick up whatever fresh, seasonal fruit you find at your local farmer's market—peaches, plums, apples or a mix of seasonal berries—any combination will work. Add a crunchy oat topping and pop it in the oven. In no time you will have a yummy homemade dessert that you will feel good about serving to your family.

Ingredients

Topping

½ cup (114g) all-purpose flour

1 cup (228g) rolled oats

½ cup (114g) chopped walnuts or pecans

⅓ cup (78g) raw cane sugar or packed brown sugar)

½ tsp. (2g) cinnamon (optional—goes best with apples, peaches and nectarines)

½ cup (113g) chilled butter

Filling

4 cups (914g) fresh fruit

½ cup (114g) raw cane sugar (or packed brown sugar)

Note: For apple crisp, add 2 T (30ml) lemon juice and 1 T (14g) flour to the filling mix.

Directions

Preheat oven to 350°F (177°C). Butter a 2½ quart (2.5L) baking dish.

Stir together flour, oats, nuts, sugar and cinnamon in a medium-sized bowl. Cut in the butter in small pieces and mix with your fingertips until well blended. Mixture will be crumbly.

Toss all filling ingredients together in another bowl. Pour into prepared baking dish. Sprinkle topping mixture over the top and bake until fruit is bubbling and topping is crisp, about 30 minutes.

Serves 8-10.

❋ **Healthy**Hints

Raw cane sugar is a type of minimally processed sugar with a rich caramel flavor. Originally popular as a sweetener for coffee or tea, it also works well for baking and can be substituted 1:1 for both granulated white and brown sugars. Its coarse texture makes it perfect for sprinkling on desserts for a little extra crunch.

Sustainable Snacks

We are a nation hooked on snacking. Everywhere we turn, we find more snacks and smart marketers have made it oh-so-easy to take snacks with us everywhere we go. Bars, pouches, tubes, even snacks made to fit in our car's cup holders are available at the nearest convenience store at any time of day or night. If you have kids, you probably don't dare leave the house for long without something for them to munch on. But what about all that packaging that ends up in the landfill?

Check out these recipes for portable snacks that let you leave the wasteful packaging behind.

Power Bites

These little snacks are packed with good nutrition and energy-boosting ingredients and are a great alternative to prepackaged energy bars. Give them to your kids before the big game or bring them to work to help you through that afternoon slump. The secret ingredient in these tasty treats is dates. Dates are naturally sweet and a great source of minerals like potassium, magnesium and calcium as well as vitamin A and many important B vitamins.

Ingredients

Cherry Almond Power Bites

½ cup (114g) chopped dates

⅓ cup (78g) almonds

¼ cup (57g) dried cherries

⅛ tsp. (.6g) cinnamon

Directions

Mix all ingredients together in a food processor until well blended. Shape mixture into 1" (3cm) balls. Makes approximately 8-10 pieces. Store in a sealed container.

Variations

Cashew Coconut Power Bites

½ cup (114g) chopped dates

⅓ cup (78g) cashews

¼ cup (57g) coconut

½ tsp. (2.5ml) vanilla or coconut extract

Chocolate Peanut Power Bites

½ cup (114g) chopped dates

⅓ cup (78g) peanuts

¼ cup (57g) chocolate chips

½ tsp. (2.5ml) vanilla extract

Go Bars

Next time you need a healthy snack to take on the go, skip the individually packaged granola or snack bars and try these yummy, homemade Go Bars instead. The easy, no-bake recipe is adaptable to your favorite combination of nuts, dried fruits and sweeteners.

Ingredients

1½ (343g) cups rolled oats

½ cup (114g) wheat germ (flaxseed meal or oat bran can be substituted)

1½ cups (343g) crisped rice cereal (use crisped brown rice cereal if you can find it)

1 cup (228g) nuts (slivered almonds, chopped walnuts, chopped pecans, peanuts etc.)

1 cup (228g) dried fruit (cranberries, cherries, apricots, golden raisins etc.)

½ cup (117ml) liquid sweetener (honey, agave nectar, brown rice syrup or maple syrup)

½ cup (114g) raw cane sugar (or packed brown sugar)

1 T (15ml) canola or other vegetable oil

1 tsp. (5ml) vanilla

¼ tsp. (1g) salt

Directions

Grease a 9" x 13" (23cm x 33cm) pan.

Mix rolled oats, wheat germ, crisped rice cereal, nuts and dried fruit together in a large bowl.

Combine the liquid sweetener, cane sugar, oil, vanilla and salt in a small saucepan. Heat on medium until cane sugar dissolves and mixture gets just slightly thick (3 to 4 minutes). Pour liquid over the oat mixture and stir until evenly incorporated.

Spread into the prepared pan. Cool to room temperature and cut into bars. (Hint: For firmer, easier-to-cut bars, press the mixture down with a piece of waxed paper.)

Cheesy Animal Crackers

Once you taste these incredible cheese crackers, you'll have a hard time going back to the box. Made with real cheddar cheese, these crackers are free of preservatives and artificial flavors or colors. Your kids can help by cutting them into their favorite animal shapes. Pack them in a snack box, and you're ready to go!

Ingredients

½ cup (113g) butter

2 cups (457g) shredded cheddar cheese

1½ cups (342g) all-purpose flour, plus more for kneading

1 tsp. (5g) salt

2 T ice (30ml) water (use only as much as needed to make dough stay together)

Directions

Preheat oven to 325°F (163°C).

Mix butter, cheddar cheese, flour and salt in a food processor. Pulse until well mixed. Add ice water 1 teaspoon at a time until dough just starts to hold together. (Don't add too much water, or the crackers will be tough instead of flaky.)

Turn dough out onto a lightly floured surface and form it into a ball. (If the dough is still too dry, sprinkle 1 more teaspoon of water over the dough and try again.)

Refrigerate dough for 15 minutes.

Roll dough out to desired thickness, about $\frac{1}{8}$" to $\frac{1}{4}$" (3mm to 6mm). Use cookie cutters to cut into animal shapes. Lay the shapes onto a baking sheet.

Bake for 10–15 minutes or until edges just start to brown. Time will vary depending on the thickness of the cracker.

Let crackers cool for 10 minutes before diving in.

37

Lively Lunches

Lunchtime is the perfect time to introduce your kids to a rainbow of food choices. Instead of sending them off with highly processed, prepackaged food, make fresh, healthy lunches they will gobble up! Here are a few ideas just to get you started.

- **Rainbow pita sandwich.** Spread half a pita with peanut butter and top with strawberries, grapes and blueberries to make a rainbow pattern.

- **Sandwich roll-ups.** Roll up a whole wheat tortilla spread with cream cheese and topped with meat or veggies. Cut into small rounds for easy eating.

- **Any kind of shaped food.** Go crazy with your cookie cutters. Create animal shaped sandwiches, cucumber stars and pineapple flowers.

- **Trail mix, yogurt-covered pretzels, peanuts, raisins or mini muffins.**

- **Dips for vegetables or fruit.**

Pack a Waste-Free Lunch!

A typical lunch box is loaded with disposables—plastic bags, paper napkins and single serving foods are to be expected. By transforming just one person's daily lunch from wasteful to waste-free, you can keep over one hundred pounds of trash out of the landfill. For more information and tips on reducing lunchtime waste, see www.wastefreelunches.org.

Instead of	Try
• Paper bag	• Durable, reusable lunch bag or box (see Chapter 2 for more information about sustainable lunch containers)
• Plastic wrap and plastic bags	• Reusable food containers (glass, stainless steel or plastic)
• Disposable utensils	• Reusable utensils (easy to find at thrift stores or garage sales)
• Paper napkin	• Cloth napkin
• Soda, water or juice in disposable containers	• Reusable drink bottle (stainless steel, lined aluminum or plastic)
• Individually packaged foods like granola bars and crackers	• Homemade versions of those snacks
• Individual apple sauce and fruit cups	• Whole fruits instead of packaged

Cheesy Apple Mini Muffins

Savory but with a hint of sweetness, these mini muffins are healthy and filling—sure to be a lunch box hit!

Ingredients

2½ cups (571g) white whole-wheat flour

1 T (14g) baking powder

½ tsp. (2g) salt

½ cup (113g) butter, plus more for tin

½ cup (114g) raw cane sugar (or packed brown sugar)

2 large eggs

¾ cup (171g) milk

1 cup (228g) diced apples (Granny Smith or Braeburn work well)

½ cup (114g) shredded cheddar cheese

Directions

Preheat oven to 350°F (177°C). Butter a mini muffin tin. Combine the flour, baking powder and salt in a small bowl and set aside. In a medium-sized bowl, cream the butter and sugar with a hand mixer until smooth. Beat in the eggs one at a time. Add the milk and mix until well combined. Stir in the diced apples and shredded cheese. Add the flour mixture, mixing by hand until just barely combined. Do not overmix. Spoon mixture into the muffin tin.

Bake 25 to 30 minutes or until muffins spring back to the touch and are lightly browned. Makes approximately 36 mini (or 12 regular-sized) muffins.

❋ HealthyHints

Here's a trick for making homemade muffins and cookies healthier without scaring away the kids: Use white whole-wheat flour. White whole-wheat flour is naturally milder and sweeter tasting than traditional whole-wheat flour but is significantly higher in whole grains than all-purpose flour. Whole grains are important for maintaining heart health, so sneak in more wherever you can!

Orange Hummus

Kids love this mild, low- or no-garlic version of hummus made with orange juice, tahini and just a touch of cumin.

Ingredients

1 15-oz (429g) can garbanzo beans, drained

½ cup (117ml) orange juice

3 T (43g) tahini

2 T (30ml) olive oil

1 small clove garlic (optional)

¼ tsp. (1g) cumin

¼ tsp. (1g) salt

Directions

Mix all ingredients together in a food processor until smooth.

Pumpkin Cream Cheese Dip

This is a great dip for apple slices. Or spread it between two gingersnaps to make a delicious dessert.

Ingredients

1 8-oz (116g) package cream cheese

½ cup (114g) canned or fresh pumpkin puree

¼ cup (57g) brown sugar

2 T (30ml) maple syrup

½ tsp. (2g) pumpkin pie spice

Directions

Mix all ingredients together with an electric mixer in a medium bowl until smooth.

Pesto

This year, try growing your own basil so you can make your own pesto! Basil can easily be grown in container pots if you don't have garden space.

Ingredients

⅓ cup (68g) pine nuts or walnuts

3 cups (686g) packed basil leaves

3 garlic cloves

½ cup (114g) grated Parmesan cheese

½ cup (117ml) olive oil

½ tsp. (2g) salt

Directions

Pulverize nuts in a food processor. Add remaining ingredients and puree until smooth. This recipe makes approximately 1 cup (228g).

Pesto Mayo

Almost anyone will be willing to eat their veggies if they have this to dip them in!

Ingredients

½ cup (114g) mayonnaise

¼ cup (57g) pesto (store-bought or homemade)

¼ tsp. (1g) salt

Directions

Whisk all ingredients together in a small bowl.

41

Chapter 2: Living

Chapter 2: Living
Nontoxic Products for Everyday Life

Stuff. We sure do buy a ton of it. Whether we live in a big home or a small apartment, we tend to fill it with stuff galore. All these products may make our lives easier in the short run, but the long-run environmental consequences are staggering. Our insatiable demand for cheap stuff has led many companies to use low-quality, often toxic materials and implement questionable manufacturing practices without much regard for the environment or human health at all. And the pile in the landfill continues to grow as "yesterday's" stuff gets added to the top.

What can we do to minimize our lust for stuff? The best thing we can do for the environment is to buy less. Take a quick look around your home. I bet there are plenty of things around that you don't really need or even use. Imagine all that extra stuff sitting in a landfill. Now imagine that multiplied by millions of households. That's not a pretty sight, is it? Next time you toss something into your shopping cart, ask yourself if you really need it. You might not.

But you can't avoid the marketplace altogether. Even if you curb your consumerism in the name of the environment, there are plenty of things you still need to buy for everyday life. The good news is, you can use your purchase power to protect the planet instead of harming it by buying ecofriendly, nontoxic versions of the products you need. In this chapter, I will walk you through the vital information you need to be a smart green consumer of those everyday living products. Whether you are buying containers for food storage, pots for cooking, toys for the kids or furniture for your home, the Buy It Green section will help you make mindful pur-

chases by evaluating products based on safety and environmental criteria. With the right information in hand, you will be able to make the sustainable choices that best fit your lifestyle.

To satisfy your creative bug, the Do It Green section includes some practical, ecofriendly projects for your home, such as sewing your own cloth napkins as an alternative to paper, making a baby toy from an old sweater or whipping up a batch of homemade play dough for the kids.

Buy It Green

When I head to the store I try to keep in mind that there may be a hidden price to pay for the things I buy, both in terms of human health and for the environment. On the health front, I may be unwittingly exposing myself to harmful chemicals through the products choices I make. My water bottle, for instance, may be leaching toxic chemicals into the water even though the water tastes just fine. And my brand new mattress may leave me sleeping in a bed of noxious fumes. Product manufacturing has plenty of negative environmental effects as well—things like the emission of greenhouse gasses, pollution of air and waterways and the destruction of wildlife habitats.

That said, I can't afford to make the perfect environmental choice every time I shop. Just like food shopping, I find I'm faced with a constant trade-off between the environment and the checkbook, and in the case of home decorating, my personal style factors in as well. I buy "green" as often as possible, but I try not to feel guilty when it doesn't work out.

In the Kitchen
Storing and Cooking Food

A typical kitchen is filled with products for preparing, storing and serving food that make life easier and more convenient. But there is a dark side to that convenience. Disposable paper products, a staple in many kitchens, waste precious resources and typically are not recyclable. Plastic products are an even bigger problem. Plastic manufacturing is a highly toxic business that produces industrial pollutants that end up in our air and water. And to make matters worse, at the end of its useful life, plastic winds up in landfills and waterways, where it continues to release toxins and never completely biodegrades. From a health perspective, chemicals used in plastic production may leach into your food and drink or release toxic fumes into the air while you cook. Fortunately, there are plenty of ecofriendly alternatives to use in the kitchen.

(a copy-and-clip guide)

Plastics Guide

Bring this plastics guide to the store to help you decide what to buy and what to avoid. Keep in mind that most plastics used for food and drink storage are classified by the recycling code found on the bottom of the product.

The following plastics are considered safest for food and drink:

Recycling code	Name	Common uses	Notes
#1 PET or PETE ♳ PETE	Polyethylene terephthalate	• Soda, water or juice bottles • Containers for peanut butter and other foods	• Clear and lightweight • Typically for single use only • Easy to recycle
#2 HDPE ♴ HDPE	High-density polyethylene	• Milk and water jugs • Detergent and bleach bottles • Shampoo and cosmetics containers	• Opaque white color • Easy to recycle
#4 LDPE ♶ LDPE	Low-density polyethylene	• Squeeze bottles for honey or mustard • Some plastic wraps • Food storage bags	• Very flexible and strong • Can be hard to recycle
#5 PP ♷ PP	Polypropylene	• Food storage containers • Sippy cups • Syrup and ketchup bottles • Yogurt and margarine tubs • Medicine bottles	• Rigid form • Can be hard to recycle

Avoid the following plastics due to toxic chemical leaching:

Recycling code	Name	Common uses	Notes
#3 PVC △3 V	Polyvinyl chloride (also known as vinyl)	• Some cling wraps • Squeeze bottles • Detergent and window cleaner bottles • Toys	• Dioxin, a by-product of PVC manufacturing, is a known human carcinogen • Additives like lead or plasticizers pose further health threats • The least recyclable plastic
#6 PS △6 PS	Polystyrene	• Styrofoam packaging • Clear, rigid take-out containers • Plastic cutlery • CD packaging • Medicine bottles	• Styrene, a chemical that may leach from polystyrene containers, has been linked to brain and nervous-system disorders • Styrofoam does not biodegrade
#7 Other △7 OTHER	Includes polycarbonate and other plastics	• Baby bottles • Water and sport bottles • Five gallon water bottles • Water filtration pitchers	• Polycarbonate plastic contains bisphenol A (BPA) (See Health Alert: Bisphenol A below for more information) • **Note:** #7 is a catchall category for all other plastics. Not all plastics labeled #7 contain BPA. If it says BPA-free, it's OK to use

Health Alert: Bisphenol A

Bisphenol A (BPA) is a chemical used in the manufacturing of polycarbonate plastic, which is found in many water bottles, baby bottles and even in the linings of metal cans for soup, juice and baby formula. The scary thing about BPA is that small amounts of it can leach out of the containers and into the food or drink inside. The problem is magnified when items are heated, which is commonly done in microwave ovens. Numerous studies have found that very low doses of BPA can lead to some pretty big health problems, including heart disease, diabetes, reproductive effects and even cancer. BPA has been banned in children's drinking products in some areas and many companies are moving away from products that contain BPA but it is still very common. Look for BPA-free on the label when you buy plastic containers.

Food Storage

Keep your food fresh and the environment clean by using nonplastic containers whenever possible.

- **Glass.** Heavy-duty glass (like Pyrex) is not only better for the environment, but it's safe in the microwave and freezer.

- **Stainless steel.** It's odor-free, non-reactive and lightweight, making it ideal for food storage.

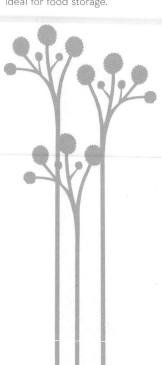

- **Ceramic.** Make your dinnerware do double duty by using it to store food in the refrigerator, too.

- **Plastic.** If you must use it, just make sure to pick a durable product made from one of the safer plastics, like #5 (polypropelene).

The Microwave

Heat combined with plastic isn't a good thing. Minimize exposure to potentially harmful chemicals by keeping plastic out of the microwave.

- Use microwave-safe glass or ceramic containers only.

- Skip the plastic wrap and cover food with

  - *a microwave-safe ceramic plate.*

  - *a silicone lid.*

  - *ecofriendly wax paper.*

  - *chlorine-free paper towels.*

✻**Healthy**Hints

Avoid plastic wrap made with PVC or plasticizers—unless you want toxic chemicals leaching into your food. Many brands now state "PVC-free" right on the box.

Cookware and Bakeware

Don't cook your fresh, organic food in a toxic pan. Traditional nonstick coatings can emit potentially cancerous particles and gases. Thankfully, there are plenty of great alternatives.

- **Cast iron.** A well-seasoned cast iron pan is as close as you can come to nonstick without a coating, but it may take some work to get there. This is one case where leaching is a good thing: A small amount of iron absorbed into your food is an added bonus of cooking with cast iron.

- **Enamel-coated iron.** These heavy-duty pans come in many bright colors. They're great for slow cooking but not so great in the nonstick department.

- **Stainless steel.** Stainless steel is super durable and noncorrosive, but you need some oil to keep food from sticking.

- **Anodized aluminum.** Known for its ability to heat evenly (less scorching), anodized aluminum is also scratch-resistant, lightweight and easy to clean. It's somewhat nonstick.

- **Thermolon.** This new cookware uses a ceramic-based nonstick surface that is completely free of PFOAs (see more information below) yet still has all the non-stick power we love. The manufacturing process is also easier on the environment, releasing 50 percent fewer greenhouse gases during production than traditional nonstick cookware. Look for the GreenPan brand in the US.

- **Silicone.** Quite the workhorse of a kitchen material, silicone is nonstick, extremely durable and tolerates extreme temperatures, making it popular for baking. Silicone is an inert material that doesn't react with food or beverages or produce any hazardous materials.

Health Alert: PFOAs

Some brands of nonstick cookware have been simmering with controversy over their use of perfluorooctanoic acid (PFOA), a chemical that has been linked to numerous health risks and has been found in the blood of 95 percent of the population. Even worse, PFOA is a persistent environmental contaminant that does not break down over time. Making the switch to an alternative cookware is best, but if you still use nonstick pans, keep in mind that they are more likely to leach PFOAs if they get too hot (over 500 degrees) or when they get old and the coating begins to flake.

Even Greener

Pick up a used cast iron pan at a thrift or antique store. You'll be saving resources by buying used, and it may even be pre-seasoned.

51

Setting the Sustainable Table

Do you serve your children meals on your best china? Probably not—and with good reason! If you're like most people, you probably start out your kids with plastic cups and plates and paper napkins. If you are loath to buy more plastic (or just sick of having so much of it around your house), head to the thrift store to buy some inexpensive but durable nonplastic dinnerware. You might be surprised to find how fun it can be to collect mix-and-match pieces for your dining table. Who knows, you may like the look so much, you'll convert the whole family! Here are just a few ideas to get you started.

- Look for small, durable stacking glasses for beverages.

- Dessert-sized plates are perfect for a child's meal.

- Collect small bowls in bright colors for snacks, cereals and desserts.

- A set of previously owned flatware is great for picnics, kids' lunches and kids' birthday parties.

- Buy mix-and-match cloth napkins to use instead of paper (or make your own cloth napkins using the directions on page 69).

- Vintage tablecloths are a fun way to decorate the "kids' table."

On the Go

Our lives are so crazy busy these days, we tend to eat and drink a lot on the run. And it's easy to rely on disposable products like plastic baggies and one-time use bottles when we're in a hurry. This just adds to the mountain of waste that is building up in our landfills and polluting our waterways. Switching to reusable products is easy—all it really takes is a change in habit (and maybe a small investment) to make eating on the go a much more ecofriendly activity.

Lunch Boxes and Snack Containers

Eating on the go can produce a ton of waste. Lighten the load (for the garbage hauler, that is) by going with reusable lunch and snack containers. Pack in a cloth napkin and some reusable flatware, and you're good to go!

- **Soft bags.** Lightweight lunch bags made from organic cotton or PVC-free acrylic are reusable and easy to tote around town. To keep your lunch cool, look for a bag insulated with recycled plastic bottles or neoprene rubber.

- **Laptop Lunch Kit.** This portable lunch kit includes individual reusable containers for packing a lunch full of surprises. A great way to promote healthy nutrition and waste reduction at the same time!

- **Stainless steel containers.** The advantage of stainless steel is that it is durable and easy to clean. Stackable stainless containers based on the Indian tiffin tin have become popular lunchbox alternatives.

- **Fabric sandwich wrapper.** A washable, reusable sandwich wrapper that replaces the ubiquitous plastic baggy and does double duty as a place mat.

- **Plastic containers.** Who doesn't have a stock of reusable plastic containers already in the house? Put them to good use holding sandwiches, crackers, nuts or whatever else you're packing. It's certainly better than wasting a plastic bag.

Health Alert:
Lead

Beware cheap lunch boxes that may contain lead. Testing done by the Center for Environmental Health (CEH) found that many soft vinyl lunch boxes contained high levels of lead. Because lead is a nervous-system and reproductive toxin, even at low levels, it is smart to completely avoid exposure to it. Be sure to check for the words "lead-free" on the label when buying soft lunch boxes.

Water Bottles

Bottled water is an environmental nightmare. Do your part by kicking your bottled water habit and investing in a reusable bottle.

- **Stainless steel.** Super lightweight, odor-free and dishwasher safe, stainless steel bottles are completely safe to use without a lining. Klean Kanteen is a popular brand.

- **Aluminum.** These lightweight, durable bottles are available in many fun colors and designs. Choose a reliable brand like SIGG with a quality lining guaranteed not to leach.

- **Hard, clear plastic (#7).** Pay close attention to make sure you're buying a BPA-free version of this very popular bottle. The bottom of the bottle should not have PC (for polycarbonate) printed on it.

Practically Green

Investing in a reusable bottle could pay you back in no time flat. Consider that an average bottle of water costs you $1. Pick up a reusable, BPA-free bottle for under $10, and you'll make your money back in ten uses.

Even Greener

Double the green factor by buying reusable lunch bags made from recycled materials. Look for bags made from recycled soda bottles, colorful recycled foil juice packs, reclaimed rice bags, recycled cotton and even old billboards.

• **Other plastics.** Bottles labeled #2 (HDPE) are safe and easily recyclable. Bottles labeled #5 (PP) are also safe but are harder to recycle. Avoid bottles labeled #1 (PETE) as they are meant for one-time use and might leach chemicals into your beverage over time.

✳ **Healthy**Hints

Don't drink water out of bottles that have been left sitting in the sun! Nasty chemicals are more likely to leach into warm water than cold.

Baby Bottles and Sippy Cups

Your baby is precious. So is the earth. Give yourself peace of mind by choosing a bottle safe for both.

• Avoid bottles made with polycarbonate plastic (that's the clear, hard plastic labeled #7 PC).

• If plastic works best for you, look for bottles that specifically state that they are BPA-free, like BornFree brand or bottles made from #4 or #1 plastic.

• Tempered glass bottles are making a comeback. Protective silicone sleeves provide baby with a better grip and extra breakage protection.

• Consider stainless steel or lined aluminum sippy cups. They are lightweight and very durable.

• Your child doesn't need a stack of sippy cups a mile high. Minimize your purchases and help keep plastic production at bay.

• Switch to a "big kid" cup as soon as possible—and get rid of the sippy cups altogether.

✳ **Healthy**Hints

Breast-feeding reduces or eliminates the need for bottles. That's truly the best thing you can do for both your baby and the environment!

Shop Green

Sometimes you can't avoid disposables. When you do go that route, look for ecofriendly alternatives like unbleached waxed paper bags, natural parchment paper and paper products made from recycled paper.

Playtime

Providing Healthy Entertainment

A house full of toys is pretty much inevitable when you have kids. But before you load up the toy chest, make sure those toys are well made from nontoxic and sustainable materials safe for both your children and the environment. Lead paint, toxic plastics, small parts—these are the reasons for thousands of toy recalls every year. Fortunately, laws such as the Consumer Product Safety Improvement Act (CPSIA) of 2008 are being put in place to protect children from many of these dangers.

Toys

No matter how hard you try, poorly made and even potentially dangerous toys will make their way into your house now and then, whether from a birthday party, an enthusiastic relative or just a bad day at the mall. When they do, use your good judgment to evaluate them for safety or check the US Consumer Product Safety Commission (CPSC) recall list (www.cpsc.gov) just to be sure. When a cheap toy breaks, use it as an opportunity to show your child the difference between a poorly made

and a well-made toy; they will grow up to appreciate the difference.

Meanwhile, you can help protect the environment and create a sustainable future for your kids by voting with your toy dollars! The next time you need a toy, skip the big box and head to your local toy shop or craft show and start asking questions about safe and sustainable materials.

55

Fabric and Plush

Soft, cuddly, squishy, squashy. Fabric and plush toys are classics for babies and little kids. But because almost everything goes in their little mouths, you need to be extra careful that soft toys are well made and free of toxic finishes or fillers. Try to steer clear of environmentally unfriendly fabrics as well, like polyester and petrochemical-derived fleece.

The ideal soft toy for your young child would be:

• covered with organic cotton, linen or wool.

• made from fabric colored with natural dyes.

• free from waterproof or stain-proof chemicals.

• filled with natural latex foam or other natural fillers made from wool, bamboo or Ingeo (made from corn).

• carefully sewn, without small parts that could come out in babies' mouths.

• handmade with love!

Wood

While wood toys have never gone out of style, the popularity (and price) of plastic certainly has had an impact on the types of toys found in most households today. Wood can be an environmentally friendly option, although it is important to keep a few points in mind.

• Look for products with the Forest Stewardship Council (FSC) logo. It guarantees that the wood used is not endangered and meets the economic, social and environmental standards of good forestry.

• Choose solid wood over pressed woods like plywood and particleboard. Pressed woods are formed with glues that give off toxic fumes like carcinogenic formaldehyde. You can check the edges of a puzzle, for instance, to see if the wood is solid or pressed.

• Look for natural, nontoxic finishes like linseed and walnut oils or beeswax. Avoid wood finished with petrochemical sealants, which can be toxic.

• When purchasing painted wood, water-based and low or no volatile organic compound (VOC) paints are preferable.

- Recycled wood is an even better way to go because no new trees are used in its production.

Recycled Materials

Toys made from recycled materials are more popular than ever. Hit a local craft show or seek out one of the many Web sites dedicated to handmade creations, and you will be amazed at all the whimsical and functional toys produced from repurposed materials. Of course, if you're the crafty type, you'll want to check out the Do It Green sections for some fun projects using recycled materials from around your own home.

Use your imagination—you could make a toy from just about anything.

- Old wool sweaters turned into felt in the washing machine.

- Vintage fabrics from old tablecloths, aprons or clothes.

- Favorite baby outfits you just couldn't bring yourself to give away.

- Clothes that are stained, ripped or otherwise deemed unwearable.

- Towels past their prime.

- Tablecloths that have too many stains to use on the table.

- Old clothes that, alas, don't quite fit the way they used to.

- Miscellaneous junk from around the house (boxes, beads, fabric scraps, buttons, plastic pots, egg cartons, etc.).

Plastic

It's virtually impossible to avoid plastic toys when you have kids. When you do buy plastic, look for high-quality, durable products from reputable manufacturers like Lego, Brio and Haba, and avoid the dollar stores as much as possible!

Craft Supplies

If you have young children in the house, or if you've got the craft bug yourself, you probably have a load of arts-and-crafts supplies around. Environmentally friendly versions of many of these products are available, so keep your eyes peeled and make the switch whenever you can.

Practically Green

Give a baby a spoon and a metal bowl. Who needs to go to the toy store?

• **Crayons.** Most crayons are petroleum based. Look for eco-friendly alternatives like soybean or beeswax crayons.

• **Paints.** Water-based paints that do not emit VOCs are safest. If you do use oils or other toxic paints, keep them out of the reach of children and use in a well-ventilated area.

• **Glue.** Stick to nontoxic, all-purpose glue (like Elmer's) and stay away from toxic rubber cement.

• **Play dough.** Most play-dough products are considered nontoxic, but it's easy and fun to make your own (see page 76 for a recipe).

• **Polymer clay.** Most polymer clay is made from PVC and contains phthalates to make it pliable. If the safety or environmental impacts of PVC production and disposal concern you, consider skipping the polymer clay or buying a PVC-free alternative such as Makin's Clay (www.makinsclay.com).

• **Paper.** Look for recycled drawing and craft paper—the higher the amount of postconsume content, the better because it means fewer trees were chopped down for your project.

• **Fiberfill, batting and pillow forms.** As an alternative to polyester, try products made from organic cotton, natural bamboo and Ingeo, a fiber made from corn.

• **Fabric dyes.** Instead of buying petrochemical dyes that contain heavy metals and pollute groundwater, look for natural dyes made from plants and minerals.

Gadgets

BlackBerrys, iPods, video-game players, camera phones—what did we do without them? Make your playtime a little more ecofriendly with these helpful hints.

• Use rechargeable batteries.

• Unplug your charger when it's not in use.

• Invest in a solar charger.

• Install power strips to make it easy to turn off multiple items at once.

Health Alert:
Toxic Toys

What parent would ever knowingly give their child a toxic toy to play with? Probably no one you know, but it can be harder than you think to monitor the situation. Up until recently, government regulations regarding toys have been mediocre at best. The Consumer Product Safety Improvement Act (CPSIA) of 2008 has helped improve the situation by banning lead and certain phthalates in products for children. However, toys made with these materials will still be hiding in the bottoms of toy boxes (and even on some store shelves) for years to come. It is important to be aware of these known toxins and to steer clear of toys that contain them.

Phthalates. Ever wonder how those cute little rubber duckies get so squishy? The plastic material often contains phthalates, a chemical used to add softness and flexibility to products. Phthalates are believed to be harmful to humans, causing reproductive problems and increasing the risk of allergies, asthma and cancer. Certain phthalates have been banned for use in children's products by the CPSIA of 2008.

Lead. A heavy metal used as a stabilizer and strengthener in PVC and as pigment in paints and coatings. In humans, it interferes with brain development and can cause problems with learning, memory and behavior. Lead paint is now banned on products for children brought into the US, but numerous violations have occurred in recent years. If you have a toy you suspect may contain lead paint (brittle, flaking paint is a sign), it is easy to test at home, using an inexpensive lead-testing kit available at most hardware stores.

PVC. PVC, a plastic material (also known as vinyl), is commonly used in products for children, including toys, pacifiers and teething rings. PVC is hazardous to humans because it contains toxic additives that can "off-gas" into the air or be absorbed through the skin. It also emits dangerous vapors called dioxins into the air during manufacturing and when it is incinerated. Unfortunately, PVC is not part of the CPSIA of 2008, but kudos to retailers like IKEA and Target who have instituted a voluntary phase-out of PVC in their stores. (You may see the recycling code #3 or V on the bottom of a product containing PVC, but there is little or no market for recycling.)

Even Greener

Buy gently used toys instead of new. Most children won't even know the difference—they're just happy to have something new to play with. You'll be amazed at how many high-quality used toys are available once you start looking.

Some of the best sources are:

- garage sales.
- thrift stores.
- consignment shops.
- rummage sales.
- craigslist, eBay and Freecycle.
- online swap sites like www. toyswap.com.
- community toy swap events.
- classified ads.

Home Furnishings

Decorating Your Ecofriendly Home

The way you decorate your home says a lot about you—not only about your style but about your environmental values as well. You can let those values shine through by making thoughtful choices regarding the types of home furnishings you buy. Whether it's a new couch, an outdoor play structure or changing the way you light your home, it's possible to decorate in a way that is both pleasing to the eye and environmentally friendly.

Furniture

Furniture is one of the bigger investments we make for our homes. Of course, we want it to be good looking and long lasting, but we should also expect it to be environmentally friendly and safe to use. The challenge is to find a piece that fits both your impeccable style and your green values.

When you're in the market for new furniture, look for these low-impact materials.

- FSC approved, responsibly harvested wood.
- Reclaimed wood from old houses or barns, factory scraps or other salvaged sources.
- Fast-growing wood such as bamboo.
- Linen, hemp, organic cotton, wool or mohair fabric coverings.
- Cotton or wool fill.
- Water-based stains and finishes.
- Plant oil finishes like beeswax or tung oil.

Shop Green

Cradle to Cradle Certified (CM) is a certification of MBDC.

A new type of sustainable certification is cropping up for furniture and other products for the home. It's called Cradle to Cradle, and it ensures that the product was produced using environmentally intelligent design can be taken apart at the end of its useful life and be reused or composted.

Health Alert:
PBDEs

Upholstered furniture is often treated with flame-retardant chemicals containing polybrominated diphenyl ethers (PBDEs) that off-gas into the air and have been linked to thyroid disorders, hyperactivity and cancer.

When purchasing upholstery, try to avoid the following:

- Fire retardants and stain-resistant treatments.

- Particleboard, pressboard or laminated wood made with toxic glues or formaldehyde.

- Polyurethane foam.

- Poorly made furniture that will quickly end up in the landfill.

Practically Green

Most of us don't have an endless budget for fixing up our homes, and buying sustainably produced new furniture is a luxury we can't always afford. Fortunately, there are alternatives that are just as sustainable, if not more so.

- **Antiques.** Grandma's old dresser has never looked so good. It's well made and considerably less expensive than a new version of similar quality.

- **Preowned furniture.** Buying used furniture instead of new is a very powerful way to reduce consumption. On top of that, used furniture has had time to off-gas its toxic chemicals, so it's safer to have in your home. Craigslist and eBay are superb resources for preowned furniture, as are thrift stores and classified ads.

- **Refinished furniture.** Revitalize your old furniture by reupholstering, refinishing or giving it a new coat of paint. People often overlook the reupholstering option because it can cost as much as a new piece of furniture, but if you consider the environmental impact, you might change your mind.

Lighting

Make the switch to environmentally friendlier light bulbs in your home. It's a bright idea and will save you money in the long run!

CFLs

Compact fluorescent lamp (CFL) light bulbs use much less energy than regular incandescent bulbs. There are many benefits to making the switch.

- CFLs use about a quarter of the wattage of conventional bulbs.

- CFLs last up to fifteen times longer than regular bulbs.

- According to the Environmental Working Group, depending on where you live, switching over two 100W equivalent CFLs will save you $60 to $200 in electricity costs over the lifetime of the bulb. Even after you deduct the higher cost of the CFL bulb, you come out way ahead.

CFL bulbs do contain a small amount of mercury, a highly toxic element. Use the following precautions when using CFLs.

- Avoid using them for table or floor lamps in places where children play.

- Recycle CFLs as hazardous waste only. Do not throw them in the garbage or regular recycling bin.

- If you do break a CFL, ventilate the area, sweep up the pieces and save them for hazardous waste disposal.

LEDs

Light-emitting diode (LED) light bulbs are even more efficient than CFLs, and they do not contain mercury.

Adventures in Green Living

When I first started to make the switch to CFLs, I ran out and bought a whole bunch of them, only to realize they didn't work for light fixtures with dimmer switches—something we have a lot of in our house. Fortunately, I found that dimmable CFLs do exist. They cost a bit more, but they will save you money in the long run. My advice? Think before you buy!

- LEDs are commonly found in bicycle lights, holiday twinkle lights, night-lights and household spotlights.

- LED bulbs for home fixtures have not gained popularity, because they do not produce the warm, soft light we prefer in our homes.

- Look for improvement and expansion on the LED front in the coming years.

Outdoor Equipment

Enjoy the great outdoors, but don't destroy it by choosing outdoor furniture that wreaks havoc on the environment. Choose deck furniture and play equipment made from these ecofriendly materials instead.

- **Recycled plastic.** Your old milk jugs can become high-quality deck furniture. This stuff is super durable and doesn't even need to be painted.

- **Sustainably harvested teak or other tropical woods.** Just as strong, dense and weather resistant as conventional teak but legally harvested from well-managed forests that work to protect the ecosystem rather than destroy it. Ask about FSC certification before you buy.

- **Recycled iron or aluminum.** Support the recycling industry by buying outdoor furniture made from recycled metals.

- **Buy used.** Prolong the life cycle of someone else's outdoor furniture and save yourself some big bucks. This is an especially good way to buy children's play equipment.

Shop Green

The Environmental Protection Agency requires a minimum of 30 percent postconsumer waste to constitute recycled paper. Read the fine print on the package and look for an even higher percentage. Paper made from 100 percent postconsumer content is available—you just have to look for it.

Practically Green

Keep a separate recycling bin for paper in your office at all times. It will help you get into the recycling habit and keep you from having to sort through the trash on recycling day.

Home Office

Creating a Greener Work Space

Working at home may save on gas, but be careful not to cancel out those energy savings by generating unnecessary waste in your home office space. Consider these steps to green up your home office.

• Digitize files instead of printing them.

• Use recycled paper with a high percentage of postconsumer content and minimal chlorine bleaching for copy paper, notebooks, sticky notes and envelopes.

• Consider tree-free paper, made from agricultural residues such as sugarcane husks, fiber crops such as hemp and flax or wild plants such as sisal and bamboo.

• Refill toner cartridges, purchase remanufactured cartridges and recycle them when they are no longer usable.

• Print double-sided copies if you can.

• Print in draft mode on your computer to save ink.

• Reduce the margins on documents before you print to get more ink per page. Better yet, change the default settings for ongoing savings.

Eco-Alert:
Paper-Industry Pollution

According to Co-op America, a nonprofit consumer and environmental advocacy group, the pulp and paper industry is the single largest user of water and the third-highest greenhouse-gas emitter among industrialized countries. Additionally, the chlorine bleaching process generates large amounts of polluted wastewater that contaminates waterways and can even affect our drinking water. Our dependence on virgin paper is also destroying old-growth forests and devastating the natural habitat for many wildlife species. Using recycled paper measurably reduces these negative impacts.

- Reuse printer mistakes and the back side of junk mail as scratch paper.

- Buy refillable pens and pencils or those made from recycled materials.

- Use package pick-up services (such as Click-N-Ship from the US Postal Service) to avoid driving.

- Cut down on paper subscriptions by reading newspapers, magazines and business journals online.

When you make your bed with an ecofriendly mattress and bedding, you are also supporting sustainable agriculture and helping to keep petrochemicals out of the environment. Knowing that you are doing your part to help the planet should help you get the good night's sleep you are hoping for!

Bedtime

Ensuring a Healthy Night's Sleep

You may think of your bedroom as your sanctuary, but it may not be the best place to nurture your dreams after all. In fact, the eight hours or so that you spend in bed each night may be harming your health rather than enhancing it. Chemicals such as flame retardants and formaldehyde are commonly used in the manufacturing of mattresses, bed linens and pillows and may be slowly diffusing into the air you are breathing while you sleep. That's not exactly the kind of bed-mate you would wish for!

Mattresses

Conventional mattresses are not exactly environmentally friendly. Typically made from materials like polyurethane foam, nylon, polyester and synthetic latex and treated with flame retardants, they are not happy campers in the landfill. They're not healthy for people either, because most flame retardants contain polybrominated diphenyl ethers (PBDEs) that migrate into the air and accumulate in our bodies. PBDEs have been linked to thyroid disorders, hyperactivity and even cancer in animal studies. Here are some better options.

- **Natural latex.** A natural latex mattress is made from rubber, a renewable resource that is ultimately biodegradable. These are top-of-the-line mattresses with upper-bracket pricing.

- **Organic cotton.** Another good choice is an innerspring mattress filled with organic cotton and natural wool. Wool is a natural fire retardant and dries quickly when damp. It's slightly more affordable than latex but still very pricey.

- **PBDE-free.** By law, all mattresses sold in the US must be flame retardant, but not all of them are made with toxic PBDEs. IKEA is one retailer committed to selling mattresses without PBDEs—hopefully more will follow in their footsteps.

- **Natural mattress topper.** If a new mattress is not on the radar, consider buying a mattress topper made from all-natural materials. It puts a soft and comfy layer between you and your conventional mattress.

Bedding

One-third of your life is spent in bed. Use that time wisely by snuggling up in chemical-free bedding made from sustainable fabrics—it's better for both you and the planet.

Look for sheets made from:

- **organic cotton.** Grown using methods that benefit the land rather than harm it, certified organic cotton is always produced without pesticides or fungicides.

*Healthy*Hints

Natural and organic mattresses are expensive, and sleeping on one may only be in your dreams. If you can't afford one, and you purchase a conventional mattress instead, give it time to air out before you use it, ideally in a well-ventilated room.

- **bamboo.** Wonderfully soft, bamboo is great for hot summer nights because it wicks away moisture and is naturally antibacterial.

- **Modal.** A fiber derived from the beachwood tree under sustainable foresting standards, Modal is supersoft and silky and more absorbent than cotton.

- **hemp linen.** This multitasking fiber makes extremely strong rope and surprisingly soft bedsheets. Hemp linen has a rich, elegant texture and is very breathable.

(For more information about these fabrics, see Chapter 5 about low-impact clothing.)

Look for pillows made from:

- **natural latex.** Latex rubber is naturally dense and makes for a nice, supportive pillow. It is also antimicrobial and dust-mite resistant. (Just don't get it confused with synthetic latex, a petroleum product.)

- **organic wool.** Wool is known for its great moisture-wicking and temperature-regulating properties, making it a superb material for pillows. Organic wool is chemical free.

- **kapok.** Commonly used as a down substitute, kapok seeds (from the tropical kapok tree) provide a soft, antibacterial filling for pillows.

- **organic buckwheat.** Buckwheat hulls make a supportive and breathable pillow filler. Full-sized buckwheat pillows are available, but you are more likely to see eye pillows (scented with lavender) or buckwheat-filled yoga cushions.

Do It Green

There's nothing quite like the feeling of making something nice for your home. You'll feel even better when you make something that helps you along in your goal of green and healthy living. Try making a reusable lap cloth for your messy toddler or a set of beautiful organic cotton pillowcases for your bed. These projects are beginner level and are guaranteed to improve your "eco-ego."

 # Cloth Napkins

Why use disposable paper napkins when cloth is so much nicer? Cloth napkins are super simple to make, and half the fun is picking out the fabrics.

Fabric quarters (also known as fat quarters) for quilting are a great way to buy a variety of prints without a huge investment and are available at many sewing and craft stores. Or dig through your scrap pile from previous projects—you never know what great napkin material you might find.

What You Need

18" x 18" (46cm x 46cm) piece of fabric for each napkin

coordinating thread

Note

To make napkins of any other size, simply add 1 ¼" (3cm) (⅝" [16mm] per side) to the desired finished size.

How to Make It

Step 1: Cut out fabric for napkin.

Step 2: Fold over ¼" (6mm) on all sides and iron. Fold another ³/₈" (10mm) and iron again. Pin to secure.

Step 3: Machine stitch close to edge on all four sides.

Toddler Lap Cloth

If you have a little one who won't wear a bib but still knows how to make a supreme mess, this project is for you! Instead of using wasteful paper towels, make your child his very own lap cloth that he can learn to use himself. It is the perfect transition between a bib and a regular napkin.

All you need is a washcloth and a scrap of pretty fabric to get started. And if you want to be really green about it, recycle an old tablecloth, a vintage apron or even use fabric from an outfit your child has outgrown.

What You Need

washcloth

piece of fabric $1\frac{1}{2}$" (4cm) larger than washcloth on all sides

coordinating thread

How to Make It

Step 1: Place fabric on table, right-side down. Place washcloth on top of fabric. Trace a $1\frac{1}{2}$" (4cm) border around the washcloth with a fabric marking pencil. Cut fabric.

Step 2: Turn fabric under $\frac{1}{2}$" (1cm) on all sides and press.

Step 3: Fold fabric over edges of washcloth on all sides. Pin and press.

Step 4: Stitch along inside edge of fabric on all sides, as shown.

Step 1

Step 2

Step 3

Step 4

Snack Sack

It's hard to leave the house without snacks when you have kids. These snack sacks are a great alternative to the wasteful plastic baggy because they can be used over and over again. Place snacks directly in the sack or, for more structure, tuck a small plastic or stainless steel bowl inside.

What You Need

finished cloth napkin made from the pattern in this chapter (see *Cloth Napkins* on page 69); for extra durability, use a canvas material.

30" (76cm) piece of coordinating ribbon

coordinating thread

How to Make It

Step 1: On right side of fabric, pin ribbon 2" (5cm) down from the top of the napkin.

Step 2: Machine stitch center of ribbon onto fabric in three places about $1/8$" (3mm) apart.

Step 3: With fabric right side-down, place snacks in the center (use bowl if you prefer), pull fabric up around snacks and tie a bow to close.

Step 1

Step 2

Step 3

Felt Baby Toy

Next time you need a gift for a baby or young child, try making a homemade toy using old sweaters that have been felted in the washing machine. Kids love anything soft and squishy, and parents appreciate a gift handmade with love. Try the lovable bunny or the cheerful star pattern, or make up a pattern of your own.

What You Need

felted sweater material

coordinating thread

natural fiberfill stuffing

buttons, ribbon, fabric scraps or embroidery thread for decoration

How to Make It

Step 1: Cut top and bottom pattern pieces out of felted material.

Step 2: Stitch three-fourths of the way around the project by machine or hand stitching. A blanket or whip-stitch, using embroidery thread, creates a pretty edge.

Step 3: Insert stuffing.

Step 4: Stitch the project closed.

Step 5: Decorate with buttons, ribbon, contrasting felt pieces or embroidery thread.

Step 1

Step 2

Note: Do not use buttons on projects meant for children under 3 years old. Small circles of contrasting fabric will make nice eyes for the rabbit.

72

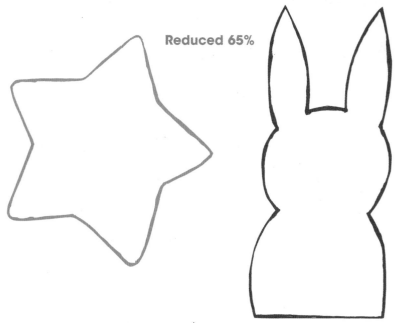

Reduced 65%

Tips for Felting Sweaters

If you ever have accidentally put a wool sweater in the wash, you know how easily it shrinks. The wool turns into thick felt that is super soft and easy to work with because you can cut it and it will not fray. If you don't have any old wool sweaters at home, pick up a few at a thrift store or garage sale and shrink away! Use these tips for felting sweaters in your home washing machine.

- Wash sweaters in very hot water with detergent, and dry in a hot dryer.

- Felting works best in a top-loading washer. If using a front-loading washer, throw in a tennis ball to add some friction.

- For a tighter felt, wash the sweaters more than once.

- Use sweaters that have a mix of animal fibers (merino wool, lamb's wool, angora, cashmere) but no more than 10 percent nylon, or they won't felt properly.

- Every sweater will come out differently. The more you felt, the more you'll know what to expect.

Felted Coasters

Whether you invest in a certified sustainable wood coffee table or just want to protect your grandma's antique, do it with felted wool coasters made from recycled sweaters. Use the simple circle appliqué, or get creative and make up your own design. (Use this same technique to make felted pot holders. Wool is naturally fire retardant.)

What You Need

felted sweater material in two coordinating colors—one color for the bottom of the coaster and the appliqué and a different color for the top of the coaster

contrasting or coordinating thread

How to Make It

Step 1: Cut two 5" (3cm) squares of felt for the bottom and top of the coaster.

Step 2: Match both squares (right sides facing out) and sew together, using a zigzag stitch with contrasting color thread, around all four edges.

Step 3: Cut appliqué piece into desired shape.

Step 4: Using coordinating thread, zigzag stitch around all edges of the appliqué to attach.

Step 4

Organic Cotton Pillowcases

A set of homemade, organic cotton pillowcases would make a wonderful gift for a friend or a nice little indulgence for yourself. Most fabric stores carry a small selection of organic cotton fabrics. Find a wider selection online at Mod Green Pod (www.modgreenpod.com) or NearSea Naturals (www.nearseanaturals.com). Makes two standard-sized pillowcases, 20" x 30" (51cm x 76cm) each.

What You Need

two 41" x 35" (89cm x 104cm) pieces of prewashed, organic cotton fabric

Coordinating thread

24" (61cm) piece of coordinating trim (optional)

Step 4

How to Make It

Step 1: Fold fabric lengthwise with right sides together. Stitch across one end and the one long side. Zigzag (or serge) the seams together.

Step 2: Zigzag (or serge) around the open end of the case.

Step 3: Fold top edge over $\frac{1}{2}$" (1cm) and press.

Step 4: Fold top edge over 4" (10cm). Press and pin down in a few places.

Step 5: Stitch hem in place, staying close to the edge of the hem.

Step 6: If desired, attach decorative trim. To do this, turn the pillowcase right-side out and attach the trim over the top-stitched hemline.

75

Homemade Play Dough

Next time your kids complain they're bored, whip up a batch of homemade play dough for some nontoxic entertainment. This version is super easy to make, and you probably have all the ingredients in your kitchen cupboards.

What You Need

1¼ cup (286g) flour

¼ cup (57g) salt

1 tsp. (5ml) vegetable oil

1 T (14g) cream of tartar

1 cup (235ml) water

natural food coloring

How to Make It

Mix all ingredients together in a saucepan. Cook over low heat, stirring constantly until all liquid has disappeared and dough becomes stiff. Turn out onto a table or cutting board and let it cool. Knead the dough until it reaches a smooth consistency. Divide into two balls and add a couple drops of coloring to each. Knead until the color is mixed well.

Crayon Cupcakes

Save up your broken crayons to make colorful crayon cupcakes that are easy to grip and fun to use.

What You Need

broken crayons

newspaper

wooden mallet or hammer

foil cupcake liners

muffin tin

How to Make It

Preheat oven to 250 degrees.

Separate broken crayons by similar colors. Place crayons between two pieces of newspaper and use a mallet or hammer to break them into smaller pieces. Chunks should be about $\frac{1}{2}$" (1cm) long and not completely smashed.

Place foil cupcake liners into your muffin tin and fill with crayon pieces. Bake for 10-12 minutes. Crayons should be melted but with separate colors still visible.

Let cool for at least an hour before turning crayon cupcakes out of the liners.

Chapter 3: Cleaning

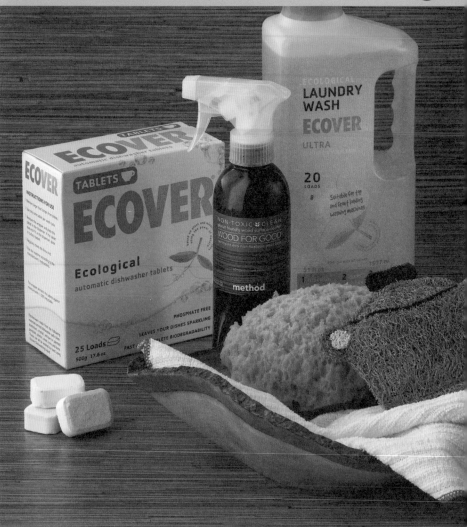

Chapter 3: Cleaning
Scrubbing Up a Healthy Home

By the time you're done reading this chapter, the cleaning products under your sink at home are going to sound pretty scary. That's because most conventional household cleaning products contain toxic ingredients that can be harmful to your family and the environment. Even if your cleaning supplies are carefully stored far away from little hands, you may still be exposing your kids to unwanted toxins in the process of cleaning your house. Noxious fumes remain in the air long after the products are used, and nasty chemicals settle into carpets, land on furniture and remain on surfaces where people eat and children play. Even worse, the indoor air in a typical American home has chemical contamination levels two to five times greater than outdoor air. Now that's scary.

As a work-from-home mom, I take that statistic to heart. I sure don't relish the thought of living in a toxic time bomb, and I certainly don't want my kids breathing toxins either. Once I realized the cupboard under my sink was a toxic waste dump, I immediately set out on a mission to clean it up. Lucky for me, the range of eco-friendly, nontoxic cleaning supplies has grown dramatically in recent years—even most discount stores and conventional grocery stores carry at least a few green products. And I've even learned to mix up a few cleaning concoctions of my own!

The Buy It Green section of this chapter has plenty of tips and practical advice for making your least favorite chore a safer one for your family and the planet. I will show you how to decipher cleaning product labels, steer clear of scary ingredients and avoid being greenwashed by unfounded eco-claims. A room-by-room tour will give you the dirt on what to expect in each major room of the house. You will also find a green cleaning guide you can bring to the store to help you make smart cleaning choices on the fly.

In the Do It Green section of this chapter, I share the many home remedies and magic formulas I have discovered in my quest for a better way to clean. You'll find some surprisingly quick and easy recipes for making your own household cleaning products as well as some simple tricks of the trade that will have you wondering why you ever used conventional products in the first place. Truth be told, the majority of conventional chemical cocktails do not perform any better than basic household ingredients like vinegar, baking soda and elbow grease!

Buy It Green

I'm not exactly a clean freak. In fact, I wouldn't be at all sorry to give up cleaning forever. That said, I have found that making an effort to stock my home with healthy, ecofriendly cleaning products has allowed me to take a little more pride in the whole process. And the more I learned about the nasty chemicals in most conventional cleaning products, the easier it was to make the switch.

The Problem

The Secrets
Behind Your Favorite Cleaning Products

If you're like most people, you probably don't spend much time thinking about cleaning at all. There's a good chance you use the same cleaning products your parents did. It's the "no-brainer" approach to a job you'd rather avoid, and that's totally understandable. But if you are still cleaning like your mother did, maybe it's time to reconsider. The chemicals in those old standbys may be good for scrubbing and sanitizing, but they are not healthy housemates. Kind of like your college roommate's creepy boyfriend, they bring along some undesirable baggage. We're talking about scary health effects like asthma and reproductive-system harm and dirty issues like air and water pollution. Perhaps we should go back to cleaning the way our grandmother and her ancestors did, using natural ingredients and muscle power instead of the chemical cocktails and wacky marketing inventions available in stores today.

The Scary Health Effects

Have you ever had a headache after cleaning the bathroom? Chances are it was chemically induced and not just caused by the labor of your least favorite chore. What might seem like a minor nuisance is often a warning sign of more serious health effects to come.

Surprisingly, federal law does not mandate health testing for the chemicals used in most cleaning products. The extent of the threat to humans is not clearly known, but the bottom line is that when you clean your house with conventional cleaning products, you are exposing yourself and your loved ones to chemicals that might cause harm. By erring on the side of caution, you lower your chance of developing chronic health problems like allergies, asthma, reproductive issues and even cancer. Take a look at these not-so-fun facts regarding chemicals in household cleaners.

- Studies have shown a link between the exposure to household cleaning products and the likelihood of asthma among children.

- Artificial fragrances, found in many cleaning products, usually contain phthalates, which are suspected endocrine disrupters.

Eco-Alert:
The Precautionary Principle

When confronted with uncertainty, environmental scientists often invoke the "precautionary principle," established at the Wingspread environmental summit in 1998. It is a common sense approach that states:

"When an activity raises threats of harm to human health or the environment, precautionary measures should be taken even if some cause and effect relationships are not fully established scientifically."

For the average person, the precautionary principle can be used as a guide to protect our health and that of the environment by limiting the number of chemicals we use on a daily basis.

Health Alert: Body Burden

It's one thing to examine the health effects of individual chemicals, but it's another thing altogether when you think about how it all adds up. The concept of body burden looks at the sum total of all the persistent, toxic chemicals that have accumulated in our bodies over time. A study by the Centers for Disease Control and Prevention (CDC) found that the average person carries almost 150 toxic chemicals in his body at any given time. Some of those chemicals have synergistic effects, meaning they create an even worse toxin when combined. Unfortunately, there are too many variables at play for scientists to make definitive connections between body burden and any specific health ailment, but many agree there is strong reason for concern.

- Volatile organic compounds (VOCs), which form vapors at room temperature, are associated with minor symptoms like headaches and nausea as well as severe problems like asthma, neurological damage and cancer.

- Formaldehyde, a probable human carcinogen according to the US Environmental Protection Agency (EPA), is used in some disinfectants and air-freshening products.

The Dirty Issues

When it comes to cleaning house, there are some very dirty issues to think about, and they don't all revolve around germs in the toilet or the kitchen sink—I'm talking about the environment. When chemical-based cleaning products swirl down the drain, they don't just disappear, they end up in our water supply and threaten the health of fish and other wildlife. Here are just a few of the environmental impacts caused by cleaning products.

- Phosphates used in dishwashing detergents stimulate algae growth in lakes and streams. The algae sucks up all the oxygen in the water, causing "dead zones" where it is difficult for fish, oysters and other marine life to survive.

- Chemical surfactants used to penetrate grease interfere with the reproductive systems of fish and frogs, causing deformities like missing or extra limbs.

- Drinking-water quality is degraded as many chemicals are impossible for wastewater treatment facilities to remove.

- Algae buildup in lakes interferes with recreational use and the beauty of nature.

Shop Green

The majority of household cleaners are made from petroleum-based ingredients. They may be cheap and easy to make, but they are not a good thing for the environment or for our economy. The production of petroleum creates pollution every step of the way—from digging and transporting (and sometimes spilling) to refining and eventually disposing (petroleum products do not readily biodegrade). And with gas prices fluctuating widely in recent years, do you really want to buy products that increase our dependence on foreign oil?

Deconstructing a Cleaning Product Label

The first thing to know about cleaning product labels is they don't tell you much at all. That's because they don't have to. Unlike food, manufacturers of household cleaning products are not required to list ingredients on the labels. Based on what you've already learned in this chapter, you know those "patented" formulas are secret for a reason.

Chemical manufacturers are required to list precautionary advice, storage instructions and first-aid advice on their labels. Keep an eye out for these "signal" words.

Danger or Poison

- Highly toxic, poisonous, corrosive, extremely flammable or fatal if swallowed.

- Even just a few drops can be life threatening.

- Found on household chlorine bleach and toilet bowl, oven and drain cleaners.

Warning

- Moderately toxic.

- Read back of label for specifics such as "highly flammable" or "inhaling the contents can be harmful or fatal."

- Ingesting 1 teaspoon to 1 tablespoon can be life threatening.

Eco-Spotlight on:
Green Seal

Look for the Green Seal certification on cleaning product labels to ensure the product has passed strict guidelines for environmental responsibility.

Caution

- Mildly to moderately toxic.

- The majority of household cleaning products carry this label (including many ecofriendly ones).

- Often indicates potential for eye and skin irritation.

- Ingesting 1 ounce to 1 pint could be life threatening.

Common-Sense Caution

- Many "natural" and nontoxic products carry this label.

- Often states precautionary warnings such as "do not take internally" or "keep out of reach of children."

Note: These warnings indicate immediate health effects only. They don't tell you what will happen with repeated exposure over long periods of time.

Eco-Alert:
POP

No, we're not talking about your dad. We're talking about something much more foreboding—even worse than a teenager running into Dad after curfew! POP stands for persistent organic pollutant, a chemical that never goes away—it is essentially the opposite of biodegradable. A POP is one that not only persists but also accumulates in body fat, travels efficiently in water and air, and can lead to some serious health disorders. It's something you don't want to run into (and it doesn't have a curfew).

Top Cleaning Ingredients to Avoid

In addition to the signal words, beware of certain harmful ingredients that may be lurking in your cleaning products. Keep in mind that because complete ingredient listings are not required on cleaning products, you may need to contact the manufacturer directly to find out what's in them.

Ingredient	What It Does	Where You'll Find It	Concerns
Ammonia	• Cuts through grease	• Window cleaners • Floor cleaners • Tile cleaners	• Fumes may cause respiratory issues, including asthma • Highly caustic; can burn skin and damage eyes • Poisonous if swallowed • If mixed with chlorine bleach, creates highly poisonous chloramine gas
APEs (alkylphenol ethoxylates) and **NPEs** (nonylphenol ethoxylates)	• A surfactant used to help penetrate grime	• Detergents • Stain removers • All-purpose cleaners • Floor cleaners • Carpet cleaners • Toilet bowl cleaners	• Disrupts hormones in aquatic life • Not easily removed in wastewater treatment facilities
Chlorine bleach	• Disinfects and whitens	• Liquid bleach • Cleaning sprays • Mildew sprays • Bathroom and kitchen scrubs • Toilet cleaners	• A registered pesticide • Highly caustic; can burn skin • Toxic fumes can be irritating to the eyes, nose, throat and lungs • Potentially fatal when swallowed
Formaldehyde	• Used as a preservative	• Disinfectants • Antibacterial soaps • Spray starch • Air fresheners (both sprays and wick deodorizers)	• Listed as a probable human carcinogen by the EPA • Respiratory irritant

Ingredient	What It Does	Where You'll Find It	Concerns
DEA (diethanolamine), **TEA** (trithanolamine) and **MEA** (monoethanolamine)	• A surfactant used as a sudsing agent • Also used for pH adjustment	• Dishwashing detergents • Dish liquids • Liquid hand soaps • Polishes • All-purpose cleaners	• Skin, nose and throat irritant • May form carcinogenic nitrosamines that can easily penetrate skin
Fragrance	• Used to scent products and mask unpleasant odors	• Most conventional cleaning products, dryer sheets and air fresheners	• Can cause allergic reactions and headaches in humans • Usually contain phthalates, which have been linked to reproductive problems in animals
Hydrochloric acid	• Dissolves mineral buildup	• Toilet bowl cleaners • Tub and tile cleaners	• Highly corrosive • Burns skin on contact • Can cause blindness if gets in eyes
Lye	• Cuts through grease	• Oven cleaners • Drain cleaners • Metal cleaners	• Fumes lead to respiratory problems • Skin, eye and lung irritant • Can eat through skin
Triclosan	• Disinfectant • Antibacterial and antimicrobial agent • Liquid antibacterial soap	• Dishwashing liquid • Some hand sanitizers • Toothpaste • Deodorant	• May disrupt thyroid function • Toxic to aquatic life • Not easily removed from wastewater
Phosphates	• Softens water	• Dishwashing detergents	• Fuels algae growth in lakes and streams causing harm to aquatic life • No longer allowed in laundry detergents

Practically Green

Here's an easy formula to remember: sun + lemon juice = brighter whites! Brighten up those dingy T-shirts by soaking them in lemon juice and water and putting them out in the sun to dry.

The Solution

The Green Cleaning Fairy

When I first started learning about the toxins in cleaning supplies, I couldn't wait to make a clean sweep. I wished I could snap my fingers and have the green cleaning fairy show up and do the job. She would wave her wand under my sink and, in one fell swoop, turn all those nasty chemicals into nontoxic, eco-friendly products that could still beat dirt, mildew and grime like nobody's business. However, all too soon I realized I would have to become that fairy myself.

Slowly but surely, I replaced my old cleaning products with safer, more sustainable versions. I found it challenging to ditch some of my old standbys like disposable dryer sheets or a bleach-based spray I thought was essential to keeping my shower stall clean, but eventually I found new products and creative ways that worked just as well and were certainly better for my family's health. My house smells naturally fresh and feels healthier—some-

times I could swear the green cleaning fairy has been there all along!

Over the years (and in the process of writing this book), I have tried many brands. Here are a few of my favorites:

- **Seventh Generation.** This privately held company based in Vermont not only makes really good eco-friendly cleaning products, they also put their money where their mouth is through eco-education, environmental activism and donations to nonprofit environmental and health organizations.

- **Ecover.** An international company with a reputation for environmentally friendly laundry products. They make an awesome cream scrub for stainless steel and bathroom tiles and a toilet bowl cleaner that makes your toilet smell surprisingly fresh!

- **Mountain Green.** This small company is known for its incredibly gentle free-and-clear laundry detergent. I love that it is ultraconcentrated and refillable. Refill pouches are available so you can fill up the original bottle to avoid the production of more plastic.

- **Biokleen.** Founded by a former cleaning-product salesperson,

Adventures in Green Living

At times I was tempted to toss my entire collection of smelly old cleaning products straight into the trash, but thankfully I never went that far. Instead of dumping unused cleaning products, take them to your nearest hazardous-waste disposal center because that's what they are: hazardous waste. If you are not familiar with your local hazardous-waste disposal options, visit earth911.com to find a drop-off site near you.

Biokleen is devoted to making safe cleaning products using natural, nontoxic ingredients. Their Bac-Out Stain & Odor Eliminator uses natural enzymes rather than toxic chemicals to do the dirty work.

- **Earth Friendly Products.** A small family business dedicated to making pure and simple products from pronounceable ingredients that are safe for people and the environment. I use their vinegar-based Window Cleaner.

- **Restore.** This Minnesota-based company takes ecofriendly cleaning to a new level by offering in-store Restore Refill Stations where you can refill your original bottles with the quick press of a button. Refilling not only saves you $1 off the price. It also keeps plastic bottles out of the landfill. What's not to love?

- **Method.** These wildly popular cleaning products work well and look cool sitting out on your bathroom sink. If you're not a fan of synthetic fragrances, try the completely fragrance-free Go Naked line.

(a copy-and-clip guide)

The Green Cleaning Guide

I recommend using this master list, provided by the green cleaning fairy herself, to guide your choices toward high-quality, ecofriendly products and avoid the greenwash.

Say YES to cleaning products

- with ingredient lists (if they're willing to state them, they're not trying to hide them!).

- made with plant-based ingredients instead of petroleum-based ingredients.

- labeled biodegradable that also provide some type of substantiation (the words "readily biodegradable" or some type of independent validation is what you're looking for).

- that go beyond buzzwords like *green* or *earth-friendly* by telling you exactly how it meets that expectation.

- scented with pure essential oils, or unscented products.

- packaged in easily recycled glass or plastic bottles.

- that are ultraconcentrated.

- that are refillable.

Say NO to cleaning products

- with the words *poison,* *danger* or *warning* on the label.

- containing chlorine bleach.

- that are antibacterial.

- that are one-time-use, disposable products.

Look for cleaning supplies that are

- durable. Skip the flimsy mop and go for one that looks like it will last.

- reusable. Pick washable, microfiber cloths instead of paper towels.

- biodegradable. Buy cellulose sponges over synthetic.

Cleaning the House

It's time to clean the house! Whether that statement evokes happiness or dread, you still need to gather up your cleaning supplies and go to it. I've put together a quick tour of the house, giving each room an eco-friendly makeover. It is loaded with advice on the types of products to buy (and what to avoid) as well as a few nontoxic tricks of the trade. You may not be able to implement all of these tips, so pick and choose the ideas that work best for you.

The Laundry Room

Wishing those endless piles of laundry would just magically go away? Well, keep wishing. It is possible to make this thankless job considerably more environmentally friendly, though. By switching to ecofriendly laundry products and energy-efficient machines, you'll make the laundry room a better place for everyone. Your family should thank you—but don't hold your breath!

Laundry Detergent

• Surfactants are a key ingredient in detergents. They clean your clothes by acting like a bridge between grease, grime and water. Look for detergents made with plant-derived surfactants instead of petroleum-based ones.

• Make sure the product is readily biodegradable.

Eco-Alert:
Optical Brighteners

Optical brighteners are additives in some laundry detergents that make laundered clothes appear brighter and whiter to the eye. These brighteners convert ultraviolet light waves to blue light, making clothes look almost fluorescent. While optical brighteners may make your T-shirt look nice, they are toxic to aquatic life and are not readily biodegradable.

Even Greener

Why use a dryer when you can harness the power of the sun? Invest a few bucks in a clothesline, and you're ready to go! If you're not partial to crunchy towels, just toss them in the dryer for a few minutes to fluff them up.

• Skip the type with added chlorine bleach or optical whiteners (see Eco-Alert: Optical Brighteners on page 93).

• Add 1/2 cup of borax or baking soda to boost cleaning power.

• Buy ultraconcentrated products. Regular laundry detergent is 60–80 percent water. Why pay to transport all that water across the country?

• Buy the largest-sized bottle you can find.

Bleach

• Skip chlorine bleach; it's toxic and hard on your clothes.

• Look for nontoxic alternatives like powdered oxygen bleach.

• Hydrogen peroxide also works to whiten those whites. Add 1 cup of 3 percent hydrogen peroxide into the bleach compartment of your washing machine.

Liquid Fabric Softeners

• Would you knowingly coat your clothes with animal fat? It's the secret ingredient in many conventional fabric softeners.

• Look for fabric softeners made from vegetable-based ingredients.

• Soften laundry the natural way by adding 1/2 cup of white vinegar to the load. It helps remove the detergent from your clothes, making them feel less scratchy. And don't worry about smelling like a pickle: The vinegar odor dissipates completely during the wash cycle.

Dryer Sheets

• How is it that we have come to think we need to throw an extra sheet in the dryer with every load? Disposable dryer sheets are wasteful and basically unnecessary.

• Try one of these home remedies instead of a dryer sheet for reducing static cling:

  • *Throw an antistatic dryer ball or a tennis ball into the load.*

  • *Dry cotton and synthetic fabrics separately.*

  • *Add 1/4 cup of vinegar during the rinse cycle.*

• If you are still stuck on dryer sheets, pick up an ecofriendly, biodegradable version from Method or Mrs. Meyer's.

Eco-Spotlight on:

Dry Cleaning

The primary chemical used in dry cleaning, perchloroethylene, is as scary as it sounds. It's a volatile organic compound (VOC) that can lead to a variety of health problems, including cancer—especially for those working in the dry-cleaning industry. You know that "dry-cleaned" smell? When you smell it, you're inhaling the residues from this nasty chemical.

Here are a few ways to avoid the harmful chemicals and excess waste associated with dry cleaning.

- *Look for a "green" dry cleaner that uses carbon dioxide to clean your clothes. The CO_2 used in the procedure is a by-product of existing industrial processes, so the impact on global warming is minimal.*

- *Professional wet cleaning is another alternative. It uses water and specialized detergents, along with professional pressing and finishing equipment.*

- *Keep in mind that just because the manufacturer tells you to dry clean, it is not always necessary.*

- *Be sure to recycle those plastic bags and hangers. Most dry cleaners will take the hangers back.*

Stain Removers

- Conventional stain removers can be tough on your clothing and on the environment.

- Look for natural products made from plant-based ingredients. Ecover makes a superb brush-on stain remover.

- See the Do It Green section for a whole bunch of ecofriendly stain-removing tips.

Even Greener

About 80–90 percent of the energy used in clothes washing comes from heating the water. Cold water cleans just as well for the majority of loads, plus your clothes will look better for longer when you skip the hot water. Bed linens are the one exception: washing them in hot water helps keep dust mites at bay.

The Machines

Washers

- Today's high-efficiency washing machines use up to half as much water and energy as older models. Look for the Energy Star logo for the most efficient models.

- Front-loading washers are especially efficient. The super fast spin cycle reduces drying time and is easier on your clothing, too.

Dryers

- If you are in the market for a new dryer, get one with a moisture sensor. It will automatically shut off the unit when clothes are dry, saving quite a bit of energy in the process.

- Be sure to clean out your lint filter after each load—it can decrease your energy use by up to 30 percent.

❋ **Healthy**Hint

Don't pay extra for sponges that claim to resist or kill odors. They are treated with synthetic disinfectants that contain triclosan and may help contribute to drug-resistant "super germs." Instead, buy plain cellulose sponges and disinfect them by microwaving them for one minute or by running them through the dishwasher.

The Kitchen

Whether the kitchen is your favorite room in the house or a place you'd rather avoid, there are plenty of easy ways to make it a greener place.

Automatic Dishwasher Detergents

- Always buy phosphate-free. Unlike laundry detergent, phosphates are still allowed in dishwasher detergents.

- Skip detergents with added chlorine.

Dishwashing Liquid

- There is no shortage of ecofriendly, biodegradable dish soaps out there—many with natural scents that won't give you a headache. They may cost a few pennies per use more than conventional, but it's a small price to pay for a healthier product.

- For maximum water efficiency, fill up two basins in your sink—one for washing, one for rinsing.

- Soak grimy pans first for faster cleanup.

Disinfectants and Sanitizing Sprays

- Contrary to popular belief, it just isn't necessary to sanitize your kitchen with fancy sprays and wipes. In fact, the constant use of antibacterial products is leading to a troublesome increase in antibiotic-resistant bacteria.

- Skip the bleach-based disinfectant products as well. Plain old white vinegar kills 99 percent of bacteria, 82 percent of mold and 80 percent of germs.

- An ecofriendly all-purpose spray will do the trick for most kitchen surfaces.

Scrubs and Polishes

- Traditional polishes often contain harsh chemicals that are bad for people and for the planet.

- Look for nontoxic and biodegradable products (Method has ecofriendly polishes for granite and stainless steel) or use a home remedy (see the Do It Green section).

Oven Cleaners

- Oven cleaners are one of the most toxic cleaning products in the home.

- Lye, the key ingredient in most oven cleaners, is corrosive enough to eat away baked-on food; imagine what it could do to your skin.

- Instead of petroleum-derived solvents, look for products that employ citrus oils or other plant-based ingredients to dissolve grease.

- Bon Ami, a mineral-based abrasive cleaner that has been a kitchen staple for eons, is a superb nontoxic oven cleaner.

Floor Cleaners

- Conventional products often contain volatile organic compounds (VOCs) that release toxic vapors into the air while you're using them.

- Skip products that claim to shine or wax your floors. They typically contain strong chemical solvents and leave behind unwanted residues.

- Plain old vinegar and water works wonders on almost all types of flooring.

- Take a pass on mops and sweepers with wasteful, disposable pads. Try a reusable microfiber mop instead.

Practically Green

Save used lemon rinds to freshen up your garbage disposal. The pulverized rinds release potent lemon oil that masks odors and leaves the drain smelling clean.

97

Health Alert:
Hand Sanitizer

While we're in the kitchen, let's talk about hand sanitizer. These alcohol-based gels may be good at killing germs, but they can have a dangerous side effect: alcohol poisoning in small children. Kids are attracted to the scents and bright colors of some gels, and it takes only a tiny amount to cause harm. A bottle of hand sanitizer is a common request on school supply lists these days, and word is that they are sometimes even packed in school lunch boxes. Hand sanitizer might have a place in a diaper bag, but in a lunch box? Not unless it's alcohol-free.

Appliances

Dishwasher

- To conserve water, scrape dirty plates instead of rinsing them.

- Try using the "light" or "economy" cycle; it may be all you need.

- Running a dishwasher once a day saves water compared to hand-washing throughout the day.

- When buying new, consider an Energy Star model—they use over 40 percent less energy than the federal minimum standard.

The Bathroom

The room where you go to get clean might not be as clean as you think. A bathroom is typically the smallest room in the house, and when you pump a bunch of cleaning chemicals into it, the air quality gets particularly bad. Steam from the shower exacerbates the matter by opening your skin's pores and allowing them to absorb all those chemicals from the air. Fortunately, there are safer solutions for cleaning the bathroom.

Tub and Tile Cleaners

- Mold and soap scum may be our worst enemies in the bathroom, but highly toxic bathroom cleaners are even worse.

- To remove soap scum and mold, use a nontoxic tub-and-tile cleaner or homemade *Everyday Spray* (see page 106).

- Stop mold and mildew before it starts with the following tips:

  - Ventilate the bathroom by opening windows or using an exhaust fan.

  - Use a squeegee or cleaning towel to dry the shower stall immediately after use.

  - If your shower has a door, leave it open when you are finished.

Soft Scrubs

- Avoid those that contain chlorine bleach.

- Look for a nontoxic, biodegradable version like Ecover's Cream Scrub.

- See page 106 for a bubbly sink scrub made with ingredients found in your kitchen cupboard.

Toilet Bowl Cleaners

- Conventional toilet bowl cleaners contain harmful chemicals and unleash harsh fumes.

- Regular cleaning with a nontoxic toilet cleanser will keep stains at bay.

- Use straight vinegar to combat mineral buildup.

- For stubborn stains, pour $\frac{1}{2}$ cup of borax or baking soda into the bowl. Let it sit for half hour and then scrub the bowl with a toilet brush.

Drain Cleaners

- Standard drain cleaners likely contain lye, hydrochloric acid and sulfuric acid.

Adventures in Green Living

Since I made the switch to ecofriendly household cleaning products, I have found that my tolerance for synthetic fragrances has gone way down. That "ocean breeze" fragrance meant to take me back to summer at the seashore is more likely to send me to my bedroom with a headache. I find I prefer the softer, natural scents of pure essential oils over synthetics any day.

- Earth-friendly, enzyme-based drain cleaners (like Earth Enzymes by Earth Friendly Products) will do the trick in a much less caustic way.

Shop Green

I'm not a fan of disposable wipes. That said, there is one area where I think they make sense—wiping the toilet seat. I'm guessing that anyone who has small boys like I do would agree. Thankfully, they make biodegradable versions now!

- Try a plumbing snake to mechanically remove built-up "gunk" instead of relying on chemical remedies.

- A combination of baking soda, vinegar and hot water works well to combat sluggish drains.

The Rest of the House

Whether you are undertaking a big spring cleaning or simply keeping up with the weekly maintenance, there are plenty of opportunities to switch to greener cleaning products throughout the house.

Windows

- When you buy window-washing spray, make sure it is ammonia-free. Ammonia is highly caustic, and its fumes are dangerous to breathe.

- Make your own window spray, using vinegar, water and just a wee bit of dish soap to clean off the grime (see page 107).

- If you don't have time to mix it yourself, Earth Friendly Products sells a vinegar-based window cleaner that works very well and is safe for the earth.

Carpets

- Most commercial carpet cleaners contain toxic vapors you just don't want to breathe. Ecofriendly versions, such as Seventh Generation's Carpet Spot & Stain Remover, are available.

- The majority of professional carpet cleaners use the same wicked chemicals. Ask around about eco-friendly carpet cleaning options in your area.

- For extra tough stains, make a paste of equal amounts of salt, borax and vinegar. Rub paste into carpet, let dry for a few hours and vacuum up.

Dusting and Polishing

- Skip the aerosol dusting sprays; the super-fine mist is bad to breathe in.

- Method makes a glycerin-based furniture polish that will help clean and protect wood without all the toxic chemicals.

- Instead of disposable dusting cloths, try a microfiber dusting cloth—it is washable and reusable.

- Worn-out T-shirts and towels make great dusting cloths as well. Be sure to dampen them first to keep the dust from moving around.

Air Fresheners

There's a huge industry built around air fresheners that claim to make your house smell like a "summer breeze" or a "rain garden," but they're actually polluting the indoor air instead of freshening it.

- Air fresheners are rarely necessary. They mask odors without eliminating them.

- Most air fresheners contain phthalates, which are linked to hormonal imbalances, allergies and asthma.

- The fine mist from aerosol sprays is especially nasty to breathe. It is also flammable.

- Safer alternatives include naturally scented soy-based or beeswax candles and pure plant essential oils used in a clay-pot diffuser or a lightbulb ring.

Even Greener

Houseplants not only look green, they may be improving the air quality in your home. Some houseplants absorb toxins like VOCs, formaldehyde and benzene that could be floating around in your home. Some of the top houseplants for air purification are Boston ferns, areca, lady and bamboo palms, English ivy, rubber plants, peace lilies, gerbera daisies and weeping figs (ficus plants).

101

Do It Green

We've been conditioned to believe that we need a "magic" formula from the manufacturer to get our house truly clean. In reality, many of the powerful ingredients for a clean and healthy home are kitchen staples, like vinegar, lemon and baking soda. Make your own magic by gathering up your nontoxic cleaning agents and mixing some of these super-powered cleaning recipes. You'll swear the green cleaning fairy must have helped!

(a copy-and-clip guide)

The Magic Tool Kit of Nontoxic Cleaning Agents

Buy This	Because
White vinegar	Vinegar is the superhero in the world of cleaning agents. It is highly antibacterial, killing 99 percent of bacteria, 82 percent of mold and 80 percent of germs. Vinegar's other superpowers include cutting grease, dissolving soap scum, removing mineral buildup, breaking up dirt and softening water.
Baking soda	A natural mineral made from soda ash, baking soda is a mainstay in most kitchens. Aside from its amazing rising properties during baking, it can pull off a few other tricks like neutralizing and absorbing odors and softening water. It also absorbs grease and provides a nonabrasive grit for scrubbing countertops, sinks and bathtubs.
Cornstarch	Similar to baking soda, cornstarch is good for absorbing oil and grease. It can also be used to make a natural spray starch for clothing.
Borax	A naturally occurring alkaline mineral, borax is a great laundry booster—it helps get clothes cleaner and brighter. It also softens water and is a powerful disinfectant and deodorizer. Use with caution: Borax is harmful if ingested but is much safer than chlorine bleach. Keep out of reach of children and pets.
Washing soda (sodium carbonate)	A naturally occurring mineral in the same family as baking soda, washing soda is a great alternative to chemical solvents. It can be used to remove wax and soot, and it also takes care of grease or lipstick stains. Caution: Washing soda is caustic, so use gloves when handling it and keep it away from children and pets.

Buy This	Because
Lemon juice	The magic properties of lemon juice include dissolving grease and mineral-scale buildup, removing tarnish and whitening clothes. It is also an antiseptic and a deodorizer.
Vegetable-based liquid soap	Castile soap or a mild ecofriendly dish detergent are helpful for dissolving oil and grease.
Hydrogen peroxide	This naturally produced liquid is known for its disinfectant and bleaching properties. As a household cleaning agent, it is effective at removing stains from clothing and mold from the shower stall.
Salt	That ubiquitous round container of salt is good not only for cooking but helps in the cleaning department, too. Salt is naturally abrasive, making it good for scrubbing. It is also a deodorizer.
Essential oils	The pure, natural essences distilled directly from plants are known as essential oils. Not only do they provide a lovely, all-natural fragrance (that beats a synthetic fragrance any day), the majority of essential oils have antibacterial properties, making them perfect secret-agent cleaners. Some of the more popular essential oils for household cleaning include lavender, eucalyptus, lemon, lime, sweet orange, grapefruit seed, pine, clove and tea tree.

Before you start mixing, be sure to stock up on the following supplies:

- Spray bottles
- Eye dropper
- Used toothbrushes
- Microfiber cloths or rags made from old T-shirts or towels
- Cellulose sponges

(a copy-and-clip guide)

Everyday Spray
(for cleaning and disinfecting)

This basic, all-purpose spray is easy to make and can be customized with your favorite essential oils. Keep one in your kitchen, the bathroom and even the laundry room for quick cleanups and day-to-day maintenance.

What You Need

2 cups (470ml) hot water

1 squirt liquid castile soap or ecofriendly dishwashing liquid

20 drops essential oil (tea tree and grapefruit seed are natural disinfectants)

½ tsp. (2g) washing soda or borax (optional)

How to Make It

Mix all ingredients in a plastic bottle. Shake well. Spray on surfaces and wipe clean.

Safe and Shiny Window Spray

Let the sunshine in with this homemade, nontoxic window spray. You'll love the streak-free shine, and you won't have to hold your breath while using it

What You Need

⅓ cup (78ml) vinegar

½ tsp. (2.5ml) liquid soap or dish detergent

2 cups (470ml) water

How to Make It

Mix all ingredients in spray bottle. For a tried-and-true, streak-free shine, dry your windows with old newspapers. A soft cloth will work as well.

Volcano Sink Scrub

This natural, nontoxic bubbly scrub will leave your sink and faucets shining bright. It will also help keep your drain clear as it makes its way down the pipes. This one's fun to do with the kids because the baking soda and vinegar foam up like a volcano!

What You Need

¼ cup (57g) baking soda

¼ cup (58ml) white vinegar

3–5 drops essential oil (try peppermint for a fresh, clean scent)

How to Make It

Mix all ingredients in a small bowl. The foaming will start immediately, so be ready to start scrubbing.

Lavender Orange Room Spray

This room spray has a light, clean scent made with naturally deodorizing essential oils. Spritz it into the air in any room that needs a little refreshing. Works as a diaper pail deodorizer as well.

What You Need

1 cup (235ml) water

10 drops lavender essential oil

10 drops sweet orange essential oil

How to Make It

Combine all ingredients in a spray bottle. Shake well and start spritzing.

Magic Potions Against Mold and Mildew

If you already have a mold or mildew problem, try one of these home remedies.

- Spray with straight vinegar to kill spores (vinegar kills 82 percent of mold).

- To help bleach stains, mix 1 part hydrogen peroxide to 2 parts water. Spray on affected area and leave to dry.

- For problem areas, make a paste of borax and hot water and scrub with a stiff brush or toothbrush.

Powerful Polishes

- **Silver.** Scrub with white toothpaste or a paste of baking soda and water.

- **Brass, bronze or copper.** Rub metal with a sliced lemon sprinkled with baking soda. Then buff with a soft cloth. A solution of vinegar and salt also works.

- **Chrome and stainless steel.** Scrub with a paste of baking soda and a squirt of ecofriendly dish detergent, or spray with straight vinegar and polish with a soft cloth.

Secret Weapons for Stain Removal

Keep this handy guide in your laundry room so you'll be ready to fight stains as soon as you see them! *Note: Check clothing for stains before they go in the wash and especially before you put them in the dryer. Heat sets the stains, making them all the more difficult to get out.*

The Stain	The Fix
Grease or oil (including lipstick)	Rub baking soda, cornstarch or washing soda into the stain. Let sit for twenty minutes and then brush it off. If the stain remains, try rubbing in a few drops of glycerin. Launder as usual.
Crayons or candle wax	Freeze the wax and pull it off. If wax residue remains, use a hot iron to melt wax onto a cotton rag.
Blood	Soak immediately in cold salt water or douse with club soda. Before laundering, soak stain with hydrogen peroxide, using an eyedropper or squeezed out of a cotton ball.
Coffee & tea	Soak stain with vinegar before laundering.
Rust	Wet the stain with cold water. Sprinkle a layer of salt on the stain. Squeeze lemon juice over the salt and let sit for thirty minutes. Rinse off salt and launder as usual.
Wine, fruit juice or fruit stains	Blot stain immediately with cold water or club soda. Before laundering, pour boiling water over the stain or apply a paste of baking soda and water and leave for about thirty minutes.
Chocolate	Soak stain in dishwashing detergent and water. Or buy digestive enzymes at a health food store: Grind up three to four tablets and make a paste with water. Rub paste into the stain and let sit for a few hours. Rinse and launder as usual.
Grass	Soak the stain in white vinegar or hydrogen peroxide. For extra help, make a paste of digestive enzymes, as recommended for chocolate.
Mud	Presoak item in warm water and laundry detergent. This will help loosen the stain. Follow with white vinegar or hydrogen peroxide if necessary.
Ballpoint ink	Soak stained area in milk or rub glycerin into the stain and let stand for twenty minutes.
Perspiration	Soak stain in a mixture of lemon juice and water and let dry in the sun.

(a copy-and-clip guide)

Chapter 4: Caring

Chapter 4: Caring
Natural Body Care

Back when I was in college, I felt like a bit of a rebel filling up my plastic bottle of shampoo from the big gallon jug at the co-op. In those days, "natural" body care was far from mainstream, and refilling bottles was almost unheard of. Not all my habits in college were so healthy, but thankfully that one stuck. I am still a fan of some of the products I discovered back in my pseudo-hippie days, including Dr. Bronner's Magic Pure Castile Soap and Kiss My Face olive oil soap bars. Those companies paved the way for the natural products industry, and now products made from naturally based ingredients are widely available—and not just at the co-op or health food store. That's a good thing because the ingredients in most conventional body care products are not so good for our bodies or the planet.

Studies have shown that much of what we smear on our skin, scrub into our hair and brush onto our faces on a daily basis is made from synthetic chemicals that can cause some pretty nasty health problems. To make matters worse, when lotions and cleansers wash off our bodies and swirl down the drain, they contribute to water pollution and interfere with the development of fish and other marine life.

Now that I have kids, I am especially sensitive to the ingredients in the personal care products I buy. That's because a child's body doesn't detoxify as efficiently as an adult's, so the same chemicals can have a more drastic effect on them. I prefer to err on the side of caution and minimize my family's exposure to those chemicals by purchasing naturally based, environmentally friendly products for our pampering needs.

But finding the right products can be a little tricky. Just because something says *natural* on the label doesn't mean it is safe or ecofriendly. You have to do a little detective work to find the secret to natural beauty. The Buy It Green section of this chapter

will show you how to be a beauty sleuth, making sense of confusing product labels and uncovering the "top secret" ingredients to avoid in personal care products. You'll also discover some tips for finding the safest and most effective products, including a list of favorite ecofriendly brands for infants, kids and adults.

If you'd rather avoid the marketplace altogether, try your hand at making some of your own great-smelling personal care concoctions, using plant-based essential oils and other natural ingredients. The Do It Green section of this chapter has some easy recipes for creating luxurious body care products that will rival anything you could find at the store, as well as some fun projects to make with the kids—like *Fizzy Bath Balls* that melt in the bath (see page 139). If you like to sew, you'll want to check out the super cute *Travel Toiletry Kit* (see page 141) for holding refillable, travel-sized bottles of shampoo and conditioner for your next trip.

Buy It Green

It can be hard to resist the pretty packages, intriguing labels and enticing promises found on beauty products in stores today. Who wouldn't want ageless skin and ultra-shiny hair, especially if you could buy it at the nearest discount store? But every time you plunk down hard-earned cash for toxic beauty products, you're putting your own personal health and the health of our planet at risk. The good news is you don't have to choose beauty over health. There are plenty of high-quality personal care products made from safe, natural ingredients. You just have to know what to look for.

Scrub-a-Dub-Dub: What's in the Tub?

You may be surprised to learn that on an average day, most people apply over one hundred ingredients to their bodies as part of their cleansing and beauty routine. Underneath the appealing fragrances and lurking behind those impressive claims, there are some pretty scary chemicals. In fact, according to a study by the Environmental Working Group (EWG), one in three personal care products contain at least one ingredient classified as a possible human carcinogen. Add chemicals that can cause respiratory irritation, allergic reactions and reproductive system damage, and you've got a tub full of worries.

Personal care products don't just coat your body in smooth perfection, they get into it. Toxic chemicals are easily absorbed through the skin and can even find their way into the bloodstream. A single exposure to suspect chemicals probably won't hurt you, but over a lifetime, these things add up. Persistent chemicals accumulate in the body over time, and many remain in bodily tissues forever. In fact, scientists have found many common chemicals in human tissues and fluids, including parabens in breast cancer tissue and phthalates in urine samples. Truly frightening for women of childbearing age is the fact that these chemicals are passed on to babies in the womb. A 2004 study by the EWG found that babies are born with well over two hundred chemicals and pollutants in their umbilical cord blood. That's certainly not a gift you'd willingly bestow upon your brand-new baby.

(a copy-and-clip guide)

The "Top Secret" Ingredients You'll Want to Avoid

Next time you are in need of a new body care product, check the ingredients label to make sure the product does not contain any of these unhealthy ingredients.

Ingredient	What It Does	Where You'll Find It	Concerns
Parabens	• Used as a preservative to inhibit bacteria and mold growth	• Found in a wide variety of personal care products • Look for ethylparaben, methylparaben, butylparaben or propylparaben	• Linked to weight gain, hormone disruption and breast cancer • May also cause skin rashes and irritation
Phthalates	• A carrier for fragrances • Also used as a solvent and fixative	• Found in many personal care products, including hair spray, perfume, nail polish, deodorant and even toothpaste • A Campaign for Safe Cosmetics study found that almost 3/4 of personal care products tested contained phthalates	• Not listed on the ingredient label, but anything that includes artificial fragrance is likely to contain phthalates. • Known to disrupt the endocrine system • Also associated with liver damage
Coal tar	• A pigment used as a coloring agent • Used as a treatment for dandruff and psoriasis	• Hair dye and some shampoos • Found in FD&C or D&C colors, particularly black and dark brown	• A suspected carcinogen • May cause skin sensitivity

(a copy-and-clip guide)

Ingredient	What It Does	Where You'll Find It	Concerns
1,4-dioxane	• A by-product of ethoxylation, a process used to make harsh ingredients like foaming agents milder	• Because it is not an added ingredient, you won't find 1,4-dioxane on an ingredient label • Look for ingredients with "eth" in the name, like myreth, oleth, laureth and ceteareth • Also polyethylene, polyethylene glycol, polyoxyethylene, or oxynol	• Many so-called "natural" products contain ingredients that create 1,4-dioxane • Classified by the EPA as a probable human carcinogen
Lead	• Used as a coloring agent	• Red lipstick (Note: lead is not listed as an ingredient on lipstick labels. Look for brands that are lead-free or made without FD&C colors.) • Hair dye (look for lead acetate on the label)	• A known carcinogen, hormone disrupter and brain/nervous system toxin • Lead accumulates in the body, so small amounts add up over time
Petrolatum	• Softens skin and makes lipsticks shine • Forms a barrier on top of skin	• Commonly known as Vaseline or petroleum jelly • Cold creams, baby creams • Lipstick, lip balms, eye shadows	• Can clog pores and interfere with skin's ability to eliminate toxins • Contributes to depletion of a nonrenewable resource

The negative impact of personal care chemicals is not limited to humans. What doesn't stay in our bodies is washed down the drain, and that is bad news for the environment. Many ingredients, especially those that mimic estrogen, wreak havoc on the hormone systems of fish, frogs and other aquatic life. Others, such as cancer-causing 1,4-dioxane, contaminate groundwater. The sad thing is that manufacturers are not held responsible for the environmental effects of the chemicals they use, so they have little incentive to change.

The Secret Behind Big Beauty

The real secret behind beauty and personal care products is that they are virtually unregulated. While the US Food and Drug Administration (FDA) is ultimately in charge of ensuring the safe manufacture of all cosmetics, the industry has been largely "self-policing" and, as a result, 89 percent of the ingredients in personal care products have never been evaluated for safety.

However, unlike the cleaning products we discussed in Chapter 3, full ingredient disclosure is required on the labels of most personal care products. But that doesn't mean the average consumer really understands what they are reading. Ingredient names are like a foreign language to most people, and it can be a challenge to know which ingredients are naturally based and which are synthetic.

Increased regulatory oversight, ingredient safety testing and improved product labeling will all help us make better choices at the beauty counter. In the meantime, take the copy-and-clip guide on page 118 with you to the store to help you avoid the most risky ingredients.

Become a Beauty Sleuth

Do you believe everything you read on a beauty product label? Let's hope not, because there are some pretty outlandish statements on some of them. Some claims are clearly puffed up, like "age-defying makeup" or "perfect lash mascara," but other claims like "natural" or "organic" may lead a person to believe the product is completely free of chemically derived ingredients, when in fact it is not. If you really want to get a handle on what you are buying and avoid the greenwashing, you'll have to do some detective work and start looking for clues on those labels.

Eco-Spotlight on: Campaign for Safe Cosmetics

The Campaign for Safe Cosmetics is a coalition of non-profit health and environmental groups working together to call for the elimination of dangerous chemicals in cosmetics and personal care products. Visit their Web site for the latest information on beauty product safety and to get involved with the campaign (www.safecosmetics.org).

Fortunately, some certifications and standards do exist to help reassure us about the quality of the products we are buying. Use the copy-and-clip guide on page 122 to help you understand which terms and seals of approval found on product labels are meaningful and which ones might require a little more digging.

Prioritize Your Personal Care

A good detective makes a list of priorities before setting out on the hunt. Here are a few tips for switching to a healthier, more natural beauty routine.

- Start with products you use the most, like face cream, body lotion, deodorant, shampoo and lip balm.

- Look for products with a legitimate seal of certification or those that list the percentage of natural ingredients in the product.

- Use fewer products. You probably don't need as many as you think.

- Buy fragrance-free products or those scented with pure essential oils only.

- Support brands that use less packaging and look for packages made from recycled materials with a high percentage of postconsumer material.

- Choose glass bottles over plastic when possible.

- Avoid products packaged in PVC plastic (#3 for recycling purposes).

- If you must buy disposable wipes or cleansing pads, be sure they are biodegradable.

- Try making some of your own personal care products (see the Do It Green section for recipes).

Health Alert: Pinkwashing

Don't be fooled by pinkwashing, the practice in which companies position themselves as advocates to stop breast cancer—while selling products that contain chemicals that may actually be contributing to an increase in breast cancer. Many conventional beauty products contain paraben preservatives, which have been found in breast cancer tumors.

(a copy-and-clip guide)

Guide to Beauty Product Labeling

Label	What It Means	Be Aware That
USDA National Organic Program	• Products contain at least 95 percent organic ingredients • Meets the same stringent guidelines as food	• Certifying agent's name and address must appear on the label
OASIS (Organic and Sustainable Industry Standard) organic	• Requires 85 percent certified organic content • A "made with organic" label requires 70 percent certified organic content	• A wide variety of synthetic ingredients are allowed
Organic	• The word *organic* without the USDA Organic or OASIS seal has no true meaning because the term is unregulated by the FDA for cosmetics or personal care products	• This is a widely overused term. For example, products made with "organic extracts" contain mostly water and should not be mistaken for true organic products
Natural	• The word *natural* on its own has no legal meaning for personal care products	• Consumers may be fooled into thinking that all ingredients in the product are from truly natural sources when in fact they are not
Natural Products Association	• Product must be made of at least 95 percent truly natural ingredients • No ingredients with any potential human health risks are allowed • Certain synthetic ingredients are allowed when a non-natural substitute is not available	• This label was created specifically for the US marketplace and is gaining ground as a leading seal of approval for natural body care
Ecocert	• A European certification agency that requires products to contain a minimum of 95 percent naturally derived ingredients and 10% organic ingredients	• Allows the use of some synthetically derived ingredients

Label	What It Means	Be Aware That
BDIH	• Requires the use of organically grown or wild harvested plant-based ingredients • Petroleum-based ingredients and synthetic dyes and fragrances are not allowed • Fair trade is encouraged	• BDIH is from the German Trade Association, and the label is used primarily by European companies such as Weleda and Logona
Whole Foods Market Premium Body Care	• All products with this label must meet stringent guidelines for ingredient safety, environmental impact, source and efficacy	• This label was developed by Whole Foods to raise the bar for natural personal care products. • The label is used for many brands sold at Whole Foods, including their private label
Hypoallergenic	• Product has a low chance of causing allergies	• The FDA has no standards governing the use of this term • Does not guarantee that it will not cause allergies or ensure that all ingredients are safe
Fragrance-free	• No added artificial or natural fragrances	• There is no guarantee that it won't irritate the skin
Dermatologist tested	• A dermatologist tested the product	• The dermatologist did not necessarily endorse the product • Does not guarantee that the ingredients are safe
Leaping Bunny	• Internationally recognized standard guaranteeing that product is 100 percent free of animal testing at all stages of development	• Does not guarantee that all ingredients are natural or safe
PETA Caring Consumer peta.org cruelty free	• Indicates that the entire company does not perform any animal testing	• Does not ensure that all ingredients are natural or safe

(a copy-and-clip guide)

Natural Beauty Basics

Manufacturers would love for you to believe that you need loads of personal care products, especially the ones that make them piles of money. But if you do your homework, you can pick out only the products your family really needs. You may have to pay a little extra for high-quality ingredients, but keeping your family healthy and the environment safe is worth every penny.

Infants

It sure is tempting to buy lots of fancy body care products for infants, but the truth is, they really don't need much. Limit your purchases in this category to the basics.

- Fragrance-free products are best for baby. If you prefer a fragrance, make sure it's lightly scented with pure essential oils and not synthetic chemicals.

- Look for products made with high-quality, plant-based and organic ingredients.

- Products like body lotion and baby powder are rarely necessary. If you do buy powder, make sure it is talc-free.

- Sweet almond oil works well for infant massage or for treating cradle cap.

- Avoid diaper creams that contain boric acid, sodium borate and petrolatum. Zinc oxide provides a safe barrier to wetness.

- Do not use sunscreen on infants under six months old. Keep them out of the sun instead.

Favorite Brands:

- Baby Avalon Organics
- Burt's Bees
- California Baby
- Earth Mama Angel Baby
- Nature's Baby Organics
- TruKid
- Weleda

Toddlers, Tweens and In-Between

Bath time is big fun for kids. Make sure the products you choose are safe for your kids and for the earth.

- **Bath stuff.** Novelty bath products like soap crayons, finger paint or bath fizzies are likely to contain poor-quality or harmful ingredients. Read labels closely and look for natural, nontoxic ingredients or try the recipe for homemade *Fizzy Bath Balls* on page 139.

- **Bubble bath.** Choose bubble bath made from plant-based, biodegradable ingredients instead of petroleum products. Avoid sodium lauryl (and laureth) sulphate and paraben preservatives.

- **Hair detangler.** If tangled hair is an issue, try a natural hair-detangling spray to help stop the tears without harmful chemicals.

- **Play makeup.** Kids at this age love to experiment with makeup, but most play makeup is made from cheap, petrochemical ingredients. Look for product lines made with plant-based ingredients. Instead of lipstick, give kids a naturally tinted lip balm.

Favorite Brands:

- Burt's Bees
- California Baby
- Kiss My Face Kids
- Little Earth's Beauty (play makeup)
- TruKid

Teens

Teens will want to experiment with personal care products as a way to express their personal style and control. Do your best to steer them in the direction of naturally based products that are safe for their skin and for the environment.

- **Cosmetics.** Drugstore cosmetics are loaded with yucky ingredients like parabens, FD&C dyes and petrolatum. Look for products made with plant-based ingredients and tinted with natural pigments. One hundred percent pure mineral makeup without preservatives or fragrances can be a good choice.

- **Lip balm.** If lip balm is in their pocket or purse, make sure it is made from natural ingredients like lanolin or beeswax and flavored with natural extracts instead of artificial flavors. Avoid lip balms that contain alcohol, which can dry out lips.

- **Skin care.** Start good skin care habits early by switching to naturally based products. Avoid harsh and potentially toxic acne relief products containing benzoyl peroxide, salicylic or alpha hydroxyl acids and alcohol.

- **Styling products.** Don't let your kids have a bad hair day. Choose botanically based hair-styling products over synthetic, and avoid dangerous aerosol hair sprays.

Favorite Brands:

- Alba
- Burt's Bees
- Ecco Bella Cosmetics
- EO
- Gabriel Cosmetics
- Giovanni Organic Hair Care
- Honeybee Gardens Natural Cosmetics
- Jason Natural Products
- Kiss My Face
- Miessence Organic Cosmetics
- Nature's Gate Organics
- Teens Turning Green (facial care from Whole Foods)
- Terra Firma Cosmetics

Eco-Spotlight on: Teens for Safe Cosmetics

If you have a teen at home, let her know about the advocacy group just for teens called Teens for Safe Cosmetics. Their goal is to raise awareness about potentially harmful ingredients found in many cosmetics and personal care products that directly effect teen health (www.teensforsafecosmetics. org).

The Whole Family

No one expects you to dump all your beauty products and start over. But as you run out of personal care products in your home, make the switch to greener, safer versions.

- **Body care.** Avoid mineral oil and other petroleum-based ingredients and opt for naturally based versions instead. Artificial fragrances are a common source of irritation with body care products.

- **Facial care.** Beware anti-aging products loaded with risky chemicals. Avoid wasteful disposable facial cleansing cloths and pads.

- **Hair care.** Look for paraben-free products that use mild, plant-based cleansers. Consider washing hair less frequently—it's better for your hair and the environment.

- **Hair color.** Look for dyes made without petrochemical solvents and avoid products that contain coal tar, often found in FD&C colors. Opt for a professional treatment with plant-based ingredients or natural dyes made from henna (a desert scrub).

- **Sunscreen.** Be sure to purchase products with both UVA and UVB protection. Avoid ingredients oxybenzone and benzophenon-3. Skip the sunscreen sprays, as fine mist is easy to inhale.

- **Deodorant.** Choose a deodorant that contains natural odor-neutralizing and antibacterial ingredients such as hops, baking soda and pure essential oils. Avoid antiperspirants that contain aluminum, which has been linked to breast cancer. Crystal deodorants, made from 100 percent mineral salts, are an increasingly popular alternative to conventional sticks and sprays.

Health Alert:
Sunscreen

We all know how important it is to protect our skin from the sun, but according to the EWG, four out of five sunscreen products either provide inadequate protection or contain ingredients with significant safety concerns. Physical blockers like titanium dioxide or zinc oxide are generally thought to be safer than chemical ingredients for sunscreen protection. However, micronized or nano-scale versions of those ingredients have been getting a bad rap as well. Before you grab a bottle off the shelf, head to EWG's Skin Deep database to search for the safest of the safe (www. cosmeticsdatabase.com).

- **Nail care.** Nail products are some of the most toxic personal care products around. Polish safely by using water-based rather than solvent-based polishes and avoiding products that contain formaldehyde.

- **Oral care**. Nix the conventional toothpaste filled with artificial flavors, unusual colors and sparkles. There are plenty of all-natural brands available that use safe ingredients to help maintain good oral health for your family.

Favorite Brands:

- Acquarella (nail care)
- Aubrey Organics
- Aura Cacia
- Avalon Organics
- Aveda
- Avigal Henna (hair color)
- Desert Essence
- Dr. Bronner's
- EcoColors (hair color)
- evanhealy (facial care)
- J.R. Liggett's (shampoo bar)
- Logona
- Pangea Organics
- PeaceKeeper Cause-Metics (nail care)
- River Soap Company
- Suki
- Tom's of Maine

Ecofriendly Toiletries

While we're in the bathroom, let's take a look at some of the other products that are often part of the daily body care routine. There are plenty of ways to make the bathroom a healthier place for your family and the planet.

- **Toothbrushes and razors.** Skip the bag of disposable razors and purchase a durable, reusable version instead. Better yet, opt for the kind made from recycled plastic, like those from Preserve, which are produced from old Stonyfield Farm yogurt cups (both toothbrushes and razors are available). When you are ready for a replacement, send the old one back to be recycled into plastic lumber for picnic tables and decks.

- **Toilet paper.** Help stop the destruction of forests by buying recycled toilet paper and other paper products. According to the Natural Resources Defense Council (NRDC), if everyone in the United States replaced just one roll of virgin fiber toilet paper with 100 percent recycled paper, we could save 423,900 trees.

- **Menstrual products.** The monthly blues are not just a curse on womankind. The environment is also singing the blues as billions of tampons and pads make their way into landfills and sewage systems. You can lower the impact a bit by purchasing bleach-free, organic cotton versions instead. Better yet, switch to reusable cloth pads or a menstrual cup. They're not just for hippies anymore.

- **Bath accessories**. Cleanse your body with natural products like sea sponges, biodegradable loofah sponges, sisal bath brushes, exfoliating bath mitts made of hemp or ayate and organic cotton balls and swabs.

- **Shower curtains.** Look for PVC-free curtains and liners. IKEA is one retailer that has completely phased out toxic plastic shower curtains.

- **Bath toys.** You know that rubber duck you've got swimming in the tub with your kids? It may be made out of toxic PVC plastic. Make sure all bath toys are PVC-free and safe for little hands and mouths.

- **Towels.** If you are in the market for new bathroom towels, opt for organic cotton—it is grown pesticide-free, which is better for the earth.

Adventures in Green Living

Sometime in the eighties, my "earth mama" sister gave me some reusable menstrual pads as a gift. I, um, used them to polish my shoes. Today I have a more earth-friendly outlook on personal care, and I opt for bleach-free, organic cotton most of the time. Who knows, I just might give those reusable pads another go.

The Diaper Dilemma

No matter which side of the diaper debate you fall on, the good news is there are many more ecofriendly alternatives than there used to be for both cloth and disposable advocates. Consider these sensible solutions.

Cloth

- Cloth diapers and diaper wraps are readily available in pesticide-free organic cotton, hemp and wool and are a great alternative to conventional cotton.

- If you choose a diaper service, look for one with a commitment to protecting the environment.

- If you launder diapers at home, be sure to use a gentle, fragrance-free, ecofriendly laundry detergent that contains no bleach.

- There is a strong market for gently used diapers and diaper wraps. It's a great way to save money and reuse resources at the same time. Check your local thrift stores or online at www.diaperswappers.com or www.craigslist.org.

Disposable

- Chlorine-free diapers made from wood pulp are more environmentally friendly than conventional diapers.

- Diapers made without super-absorbent gel are available for those who want to go completely chemical free. Tushies is a popular brand.

In-Between

- Hybrid isn't just for cars anymore—it is all the rage in the world of baby diapers. Hybrid diaper products, such as gDiapers, are a blend of cloth and disposables. They consist of disposable liners inside a washable cotton diaper "pant." The liners are flushable, and you can even compost the wet ones.

- Many people choose to take the middle road and use cloth diapers at home and disposables when out and about.

Wipes

- Biodegradable, fragrance-free versions are better for both your baby and the earth.

- Look for wipes bleached with hydrogen peroxide instead of chlorine.

- Buy refill packs instead of a new dispenser tub each time.

- Make your own reusable wipes using cotton flannel and homemade wipe solution (see directions on page 140).

Do It Green

Making your own body care products probably sounds better than ever now that you know what's in some of the stuff you buy from the store. The homemade products in this chapter contain fewer ingredients than their commercially prepared counterparts, and they weren't cooked up in some high-tech chemistry lab, either. Instead, they are made with natural ingredients that are nourishing to the skin and friendly to the environment.

Whether it's for a special gift, a project for teenagers to make with friends or a little indulgence for yourself, these homemade products fit the bill. After you get the basics down, you'll probably want to experiment and mix up some body care concoctions of your own!

If you still need convincing, here are a few more reasons to say goodbye to the cosmetics counter and hello to homemade.

- **You control the ingredients.**

- **You choose your favorite scents.**

- **You save money over pricey brands.**

- **You save resources by reusing containers.**

- **They make great gifts.**

- **Making your own is creative and fun!**

The Home Apothecary

Many of the natural ingredients in these recipes, including baking soda, honey and cocoa powder, can be found in your kitchen cupboard. Other ingredients, such as shea butter, beeswax and various carrier oils, can be found at natural food stores, co-ops or online retailers (see the Resources section on page 206 for details).

Carrier oils. Carrier oils—derived from the seeds and nuts of plants, fruits and vegetables—provide the base for many skin care products. Look for oils that have been expeller pressed or cold pressed as opposed to those that have been extracted using chemicals. Sweet almond oil, jojoba oil, avocado oil, olive oil, coconut oil and apricot kernel oil are some of the most popular carrier oils.

Essential oils. Essential oils are pure, natural oils distilled from the flowers, leaves, roots, seeds and resins of plants. They have been used for medicinal purposes since the time of the ancient Egyptians and are known for their antiseptic, antibiotic, anti-inflammatory and rejuvenating properties. The small molecular structure of essential oils allows them to easily penetrate the skin, making them valuable therapeutic skin care ingredients. Soothing oils include lavender, sandalwood, geranium, rose and chamomile. Energizing oils include peppermint, rosemary, eucalyptus and citrus oils. A note of caution: Essential oils are highly concentrated. Always dilute an essential oil before using it on your skin.

Castile soap. A very gentle, vegetable oil-based soap. Works well as a base for shampoo or bubble bath.

Cocoa butter. A very rich, emollient "butter" derived from cocoa beans. It is hard at room temperature but melts when applied to warm skin.

Shea butter. A natural fat extracted from the nuts of the karate tree in Africa, shea butter is a fantastic skin softener. Unrefined shea butter is yellowish in color and has a naturally nutty, smoky smell. Refined shea butter is white and odorless, but most brands use chemical solvents to create it.

Beeswax. A natural emulsifier that helps seal in hydration and is great for making moisturizing lip balms. Look for unrefined, unbleached beeswax that is naturally yellow in color.

Epsom salt (magnesium sulfate). A pure mineral salt known to reduce swelling and inflammation, Epsom salt is great for soothing aching muscles.

Citric acid. A naturally occurring acid used as a water softener in bath products, citric acid produces natural fizzy bubbles when combined with baking soda and water.

Adventures in Green Living

I've never been much of a perfume wearer; most of them are so strong they give me a headache. But I do enjoy just a bit of a scent lingering after a shower, whether it is from my body lotion, bath soap or hair conditioner. That's why I appreciate the nice subtle, natural scents of pure essential oils. They linger just long enough without being overpowering (except for patchouli oil, which is famous for its strong and lasting scent).

135

Sensuous Shea Butter Body Cream

Shea butter makes this body cream luxuriously soft and rich. A blend of essential oils gives it a warm, sensuous scent.

What You Need

3 T (43g) shea butter

4 T (60ml) sweet almond oil

8 drops each geranium, orange and sandalwood essential oils

How to Make It

Heat the shea butter in a double boiler until melted. Stir in the sweet almond oil. Remove from heat and stir in the essential oils. Pour into a glass container. Apply liberally to dry skin.

Vanilla Sugar Body Scrub

Why pay big bucks for a department store body scrub when you can make a homemade version in minutes? Sugar cane produces glycolic acid, a natural alpha hydroxy acid that helps dissolve dead skin cells, leaving skin feeling incredibly soft and smooth. The large granules of raw cane sugar give it extra polishing power, and the vanilla scent will leave you smelling lightly sweet. Package it up with a ribbon and a decorative label for a wonderful gift!

What You Need

1 cup (228g) raw cane sugar

½ cup (117ml) sweet almond oil (can substitute sesame oil, apricot kernel oil, coconut oil or olive oil)

1 tsp. (5ml) vanilla extract

How to Make It

Mix all ingredients in a small bowl. Massage scrub onto wet skin in shower or bath. Rinse. Store scrub in a glass jar. Refrigeration is not required, but product should be used within 6 months to ensure freshness.

Orange Almond Facial Scrub

Almond meal gently exfoliates dead skin cells, while honey moisturizes. Fresh orange juice adds natural antioxidants to nourish and protect skin.

What You Need

2 T (28g) finely ground almonds or almond meal

1 T (15ml) honey

1½ tsp. (7ml) fresh orange juice

Pinch of orange zest (optional)

How to Make It

Mix all ingredients in a small bowl. Massage scrub into face and throat. Rinse. Makes one application.

Chocolate Facial Mask

This facial mask not only smells incredible (and, yes, you can eat it), but it will leave your face wonderfully soft and smooth. Cocoa powder provides antioxidant properties that help protect skin from free radicals. Honey is a natural humectant, and yogurt adds lactic acid to help dissolve dead skin cells.

What You Need

2 T (28g) unsweetened cocoa powder

2 T (30ml) plain yogurt

1 T (15ml) honey

How to Make It

Mix all ingredients in a small bowl. Apply to face and neck, avoiding eye area. Kick back, relax and enjoy the delicious aroma for about 15 minutes. Rinse off with warm water. Makes one application.

Peppermint Foot Cream

This blend of cocoa butter, beeswax and jojoba oil will provide needed moisture, and the tingle of peppermint oil will invigorate tired and achy feet.

What You Need

¼ cup (57g) cocoa butter

2 T (28g) beeswax

2 T (30ml) jojoba oil

30 drops peppermint essential oil

How to Make It

Heat cocoa butter and beeswax in the top of a double boiler until melted. Add jojoba oil. Remove from heat and add peppermint oil. Mix well and pour into glass or tin container. Cream will harden in cool weather but will melt when applied to warm skin.

Luscious Lip Balm

Your lips will love this soothing and refreshing lip balm. Shea butter softens, while beeswax gives the balm "sticking power." Customize it with your favorite flavor.

What You Need

1 T (14g) beeswax

1 T (14g) shea butter

1 T (15ml) sweet almond oil

20 drops essential oil (peppermint, grapefruit and lime are popular flavors)

How to Make It

Heat the beeswax and shea butter in a double boiler until melted. Stir in sweet almond oil. Remove from heat and stir in the essential oil. Quickly pour into tins, jars or tubes. Allow to set. Makes three or four lip balms, depending on size of container.

Fizzy Bath Balls

What child wouldn't love something fizzy in the tub? These Fizzy Bath Balls are easy to make with kids, and the natural ingredients make them safe for even the most delicate skin. Try them as a fun birthday party or playdate activity!

What You Need

1 cup (228g) baking soda

½ cup (114g) cornstarch

½ cup (114g) citric acid

⅛ cup (29g) Epsom salts

¾ T (10ml) water

2½ T (37ml) carrier oil (grapeseed, sunflower or sweet almond oil)

10–20 drops essential oil

3–4 drops natural food coloring (optional)

Mold (molds are available in craft stores, but ice cube trays and ice cream or melon scoops work as well)

How to Make It

Sift baking soda, cornstarch and citric acid in a glass bowl. Add Epsom salts to mixture and whisk well.

Mix water, oil and essential oil (and coloring if using) in a small jar. Slowly drizzle wet ingredients over dry ingredients, mixing constantly to keep the fizzy reaction from starting. The mixture will be very dry and crumbly.

Press mixture together into 1"-2" (3cm–5cm) balls. Balls can be free-form or pressed into molds.

If using molds, let rest for a few minutes and then unmold. Place balls on a waxed paper-covered baking sheet and allow to dry for about 48 hours.

Popular Scents

Single scents like tangerine, lavender or peppermint are nice or make one of the following blends:

Sleepytime

10 drops Roman chamomile

10 drops lavender

Stress Relief

8 drops lavender

6 drops sandalwood

6 drops neroli

Citrus Punch

8 drops lemon

6 drops orange

6 drops lime

Practically Green

Save money and resources by making these products yourself instead of buying expensive prepackaged versions at the store. Many co-ops and natural food stores sell unscented base products in bulk, including castile soap, bath salts and carrier oils.

- **Bubble bath.** Purchase unscented castile soap and scent it with your own essential oils at home. For a moisturizing bath, add 1 teaspoon (5ml) of natural vegetable glycerin to the bath water.

- **Oatmeal bath.** An oatmeal bath is commonly prescribed by doctors for eczema, diaper rash, dry skin and chicken pox. Instead of buying individual packets of colloidal oatmeal bath, simply grind up oatmeal (quick oats or regular) in a food processor until it is a very fine powder. Sprinkle $1/3$ cup (75ml) of the oat powder into the bath. Make sure it is well distributed. Soak for 15–20 minutes.

- **Bath salts.** Unscented Epsom salts are inexpensive and easy to find. Use pure essential oils to create your favorite scent. Add baking soda ($1/2$ cup [114g] per bath) to help soften the water and your skin.

- **Herbal bath.** Put a handful of dried herbs or flower petals into a muslin bag or cheesecloth and allow to steep in warm bathwater. Lavender, chamomile and rose are relaxing, while peppermint, rosemary and basil will energize and stimulate circulation.

- **Massage oil.** Create your favorite essential oil blend and add it to the unscented carrier oil of your choice.

- **Soap balls.** Save those little bits and pieces of soap that are too small to use. Use a cheese grater to grate the soap bits into a bowl. Add a few drops of essential oil and just enough warm water for them to stick together. Mix ingredients thoroughly and press into balls. Allow to air-dry completely before using.

 # Homemade Wipes

Reusable wipes are better for the planet and extra gentle on your baby's bottom.

What You Need

8–12 small washcloths or strips of cotton flannel

Empty container with a lid (recycle a disposable wipes container if you have one)

Wipes solution: 3 cups (705ml) water, $1/8$ cup (29ml) olive oil, 1 T (15ml) liquid castile soap

How to Make It

Place wipes in container. Mix wipes solution in a small bowl. Pour solution over wipes to moisten. Keep in closed container.

Travel Toiletry Kit

Instead of buying brand new, plastic travel-sized bottles of toiletries every time you run out, keep refillable bottles on hand. This practical but adorable toiletry kit will make it easy to want to reuse instead of buying new.

What You Need

2 11" × 19" (28cm × 48cm) pieces of fabric (waterproof, PVC-free vinyl fabric works best because it can be wiped clean, but any durable cotton fabric will also work)

Coordinating thread

36" (91cm) piece of coordinating ribbon

How to Make It

Step 1: Match the two pieces of fabric together with right sides facing in. Using a $1/2$" (1 cm) seam allowance, sew around the edges, leaving a 4" (10cm) opening along one side. Reinforce the corners by stitching over the same area again. Clip the corners.

Step 2: Turn right-side out and press. (If using vinyl, place a towel between iron and fabric and iron on very low setting.) Hand stitch the opening closed.

Step 3: Fold up one short end so the project is in thirds (approximately 6" [15cm]). Stitch the sides together.

Step 4: Make three pockets by stitching two straight lines through the folded material.

Step 5: Sew ribbon onto the top of the toiletry kit with 13" (33cm) below the seam and 23" (58cm) above.

Chapter 5: Wearing

Chapter 5: Wearing
Low Impact Clothing

The change of the seasons typically means I get out the boxes of my kids' clothes to find out what still fits and then figure out what I need to buy to round out their wardrobes for the next few months. I'm the nostalgic type, so I'm sometimes a bit wistful when I realize they've outgrown a favorite shirt or pair of pants. But after I get over those crazy "Can't they stay small forever?" sentiments, I typically end up with four piles of clothes—keep, consign, donate and craft. With two rough-and-tumble boys, I don't usually end up with much clothing worthy of the consignment shops, so most of our used clothes are either handed down to friends or dropped off at the thrift shop. The craft pile is my inspiration for future projects.

As you cull through your family's closets and dressers each season, you'll no doubt find you'll need (and want) to buy a few new things. This might be a good time to think about how you spend your clothing dollars. Do you spend them on conventional clothing produced using pesticide-heavy fabrics or petrochemically derived synthetics? Do you stock up on fashion-forward duds that may last only a few months before they are destined for the

fashion dump? If so, it might be time for a change, even if it's just a few pieces of clothing at a time.

You'll be well on your way to making that change after reading the Buy It Green section of this chapter. Learn which fabrics are better for the earth and why, familiarize yourself with the eco-labels you may find on clothing and read up on buying strategies that will help reduce your impact on the environment and on your wallet.

If you're the creative type, there are loads of things you can do to either extend the life of old clothing or give worn-out items a new life. The Do It Green section is filled with fun projects that will get your creative juices flowing. Not only will you end up with unique, handcrafted items to keep or give away, you will be rescuing old clothes from the garbage heap to boot!

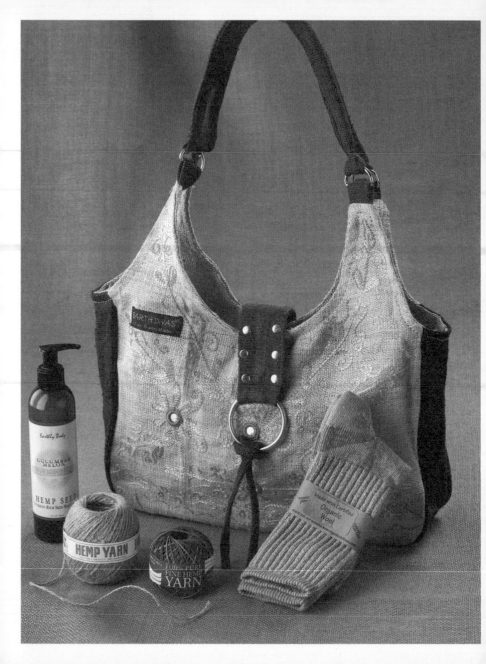

Buy It Green

When I do head to the store to buy new clothes, I try hard not to be sucked into buying the latest, cheapest fashions. Instead I look for high-quality, versatile pieces that will still be in fashion next year and the year after. My eco-radar is always on, searching for clothing made from earth-friendly fabrics like organic cotton or hemp. My conscience feels best when I buy from companies that follow fair trade principles instead of those that utilize sweatshops to make their goods. If you're like me, you can't afford the organic and fair trade versions every time, but know that each time you do choose to spend your clothing dollars on a sustainable alternative, it makes a difference in the world.

Toxic Textiles

The textile industry produces more than just textiles; it produces a ton of pollution and requires toxic chemicals that take a heavy toll on the environment and humans alike. On the environmental front, clothing factories discharge large amounts of contaminated wastewater into streams and rivers and spew a variety of chemicals into the air. Additional waste materials from the production process are dumped into landfills where they sit—forever.

From a human perspective, the textile industry is equally scary. Pesticide poisoning causes many thousands of deaths each year, especially in developing countries, and a high percentage of cotton workers develop health problems, including neurological and vision disorders. Factory workers come in contact with numerous hazardous chemicals like bleaches, dyes, glues and finishing chemicals that can burn skin and be toxic to breathe in. It's not a pretty picture, certainly not one you would find on the cover of a fashion magazine.

Eco-Spotlight on:
American Apparel

American Apparel, a popular purveyor of T-shirts and fashion clothing, has joined forces with the Sustainable Cotton Project, a nonprofit group dedicated to increasing the amount of organic cotton grown in California. By making the commitment to purchase Cleaner Cotton for many of their products, American Apparel is hoping to help farmers reduce chemical use without resorting to genetically modified cottonseeds.

The Cotton Conundrum

Our beloved cotton shirts may be nice and soft, but it takes a boatload of chemicals to make them. Here are a few reasons why conventional cotton production is not so good for the planet.

• It takes $1/3$ pound of pesticides and synthetic fertilizers to produce one cotton T-shirt.

• The World Health Organization estimates that at least three million people are poisoned by pesticides each year. Many of them are children.

• Runoff from cotton fields contaminates drinking water and freshwater resources.

• Pesticide spray is blown by winds and kills birds, butterflies and other wildlife.

• Pesticide-laden cottonseed is used as a source of feed for cattle. Residues build up in the fatty tissues of animals and show up in the meat and dairy products we eat.

• Over 60 percent of American-grown cotton is genetically engineered. It is developed to survive huge amounts of toxic herbicides, and some even exude their own insecticides.

The Synthetic Story

Man-made, synthetic fabrics may be strong and durable, but they are made from nonrenewable resources and leave behind a large environmental footprint.

• Polyester and nylon are derived from crude oil in an energy-intensive, emission-spewing process.

• Acrylic is also derived from fossil fuels and is made from acrylonitrile, a probable carcinogen.

• Rayon starts with natural wood cellulose but requires a chemical-laden viscose process to turn it into usable fiber. Rayon fabric usually requires dry cleaning, another environmental no-no.

• Man-made fibers are not biodegradable, so they'll be on the planet forever.

- On a positive note, recycled polyester requires fewer resources to produce than brand new cotton fiber.

Dangerous Dyes

Traditional chemical dyes used to color fabrics can cause allergic reactions, headaches and nausea in some people. They are bad for the environment, too, creating toxic wastewater that pollutes rivers and streams. Here are some better alternatives.

- Dyes made from organic material like tree bark, plant roots, nuts or onion skins.

- Fiber-reactive dyes that bond with fabric, rather than coat it—the process uses less water and energy, making it more ecofriendly than traditional dyes.

- Fabric bleached with hydrogen peroxide rather than chlorine bleach.

- Undyed fabric in a variety of natural hues.

Funky Finishes

Specialized fabric finishes are usually made with risky chemicals likely to cause harm to the environment and humans. If you do buy treated clothes, wash them before wearing to help lower exposure to unwanted chemicals.

- Waterproof and stain-repellent products are often made with perfluorinated compounds (PFCs).

Health Alert: Sweatshop Labor

If you buy clothes in traditional apparel stores, it is very likely they were produced using sweatshop labor. In developing nations it is not uncommon for children to work thirteen hours or more per day, enduring unhealthy—even dangerous—working conditions while earning extremely low wages. That's a high price to pay for fashion, and we shouldn't tolerate it.

What can you do other than go naked? Let your favorite clothing retailer know you want change by filling out a customer comment card or sending them an online message asking for fair wages and conditions for workers. Meanwhile, contribute your clothing dollars to retailers that sell fair trade clothing to ensure the workers who made your new shirt were treated fairly and paid a living wage. Check out the following resources for fair trade and sweatshop-free apparel:

- Fair Trade Federation (click on Find Products): http://fairtradefederation.org

- Co-op America's National Green Pages: www.coopamerica.org

- No Sweat Apparel: www.nosweatapparel.com

These nasty chemicals are persistent in the environment and are potent greenhouse gasses.

- All loose-fitting children's pajamas must be treated with chemical flame retardants to meet US flammability standards. These chemicals accumulate in people, animals and the environment and have been linked to nervous and reproductive system disruptions. Avoid flame retardants by purchasing snug-fitting 100 percent organic cotton pajamas instead.

- Wrinkle-free treatments such as permanent press may contain formaldehyde—you know, the stuff used to preserve science experiments.

Eco-Spotlight on:
Fair Indigo

The people behind Fair Indigo, a company that produces fair trade clothing and accessories, were determined to pioneer a change in the clothing industry. They left their jobs in the traditional apparel industry and started a company committed to putting people before profit by ensuring fair wages and conditions for all workers. They do this by developing long-lasting partnerships with worker-owned cooperatives and small, family-owned factories around the world. View their handiwork at www.fairindigo.com.

- Avoid rain gear made with PVC plastic. If it has that familiar plastic smell, it is releasing toxic fumes.

- Many fabric finishes are created using nanotechnology to permanently alter the fabric. Nanoparticles are so teeny-tiny they may be absorbed into the skin and bloodstream.

Eco-fashion Finds

It's easy to be discouraged when reading about the many faux pas of the fashion industry. Toxic chemicals, over-the-top marketing tactics, sweatshop labor—kind of makes you want to move to a beach town where clothing is minimal (or optional) and there's no need to shop at all. Barring complete removal from civilized society, you'll need to make peace with your purchases and find a balance of affordable, ecofriendly choices and your own personal style.

Fortunately, earth-friendly fashion is not just for hippies anymore. Gone are the days of itchy hemp sweaters or jute shoes that cut into your feet. These days you can find a wide assortment of sustainably produced clothing, shoes, jewelry and accessories at specialty stores and discount stores alike. You'll feel good in your skin in more ways than one!

Sustainable Clothing Standards

Wondering if your favorite shirt is truly environmentally friendly? Concerned about fabrics or finishes that might irritate your child's skin? Textile industry practices are not as transparent as one would like, but there are some certifications you can look for on the label or hang-tag to guide you in the right direction.

(a copy-and-clip guide)

Label	What It Means	Be Aware That
Standard clothing label	A standard label is required for all manufactured clothing that includes the fiber content, the name of the country where the product was manufactured and care instructions	• *Made in USA* means fewer transportation miles and typically better conditions for workers • Think twice when you see *Dry Clean Only* on a label. Conventional dry cleaning is not an earth-friendly process
Global Organic Textile Standard (GOTS)	This relatively new standard ensures the organic status of textiles every step of the way—from raw materials to production, processing, packaging and labeling	• Includes requirements for environmental and socially responsible manufacturing processes
Oeko-Tex Standard 100	Oeko-Tex is an international certification program that tests for more than one hundred harmful substances, such as formaldehyde, pesticides and heavy metals	• Provides uniform standards throughout the manufacturing chain to ensure the clothing is safe and skin-friendly
Fair Trade Federation	Members of the Fair Trade Federation have committed to selling only items sourced according to fair trade principles of reasonable wages, environmental sustainability, cultural respect and building long-term relationships	• There is currently no independent third-party certification for fair trade apparel; however the Fair Trade Federation works with businesses that sell fair trade clothing and accessories, among other products
National USDA Organic Program	Textiles with this seal must meet the same stringent guidelines as all other agricultural products	• Standards cover raw fiber only and don't include fabric dyes and finishes • Does not necessarily ensure an environmentally friendly manufacturing process

Adventures in Green Living

Should we feel guilty for every nonorganic cotton shirt we buy? Of course not! But having the awareness helps us make better choices when we can. My strategy? I hit the sale rack at stores that carry the good, ecofriendly stuff, look for online deals at my favorite sites and buy used whenever possible.

Earth-Friendly Fabrics

As you wear out or grow out of pieces in your wardrobe, consider replacing those pieces with clothes made from the following fabrics. Check the tag to add some green to your style.

Organic Cotton

Organic cotton is grown without pesticides, herbicides, insecticides or fungicides.

• Instead, pest and weed control methods like cover crop rotations and compost are used to replenish soil fertility with a minimal impact on the environment.

• Beneficial insects and trap crops are healthier ways to manage pests than spraying pesticides.

• Genetically modified seeds are not allowed.

• Third-party certification organizations like the USDA National Organic Program and the Global Organic Textile Standard verify that proper production methods and materials are used.

• Organic cotton is often blended with other natural fibers like hemp, bamboo or soy.

• Demand for organic clothing has been skyrocketing but still accounts for less than 1 percent of the world's cotton crop.

Hemp

Despite the association with its illegal cousin, you will never be arrested for owning a hemp sweater.

• Hemp has superpowers of its own:

 • Naturally resists pests and weeds.

 • Produces two to three times more fiber per acre than cotton.

 • Is four times stronger than cotton and has been used to make rope for centuries.

 • Grows quickly.

- Hemp fabric blocks up to 95 percent of UV rays and is naturally fire retardant.

- Its durability makes it especially nice for shoes and handbags.

- Hemp is easy to dye and retains color well.

Organic Linen

Linen is a natural fiber made from the flax plant.

- Organic linen is grown without pesticides or herbicides, and even nonorganic linen uses considerably fewer pesticides than cotton.

- Known for its durability, linen is two to three times stronger than cotton.

- Linen fabric helps keep you cool.

Wool

Wool is warm, moisture-regulating and antimicrobial.

- Merino wool is known for its exceptional softness.

- Organically produced wool skips the toxic parasiticides, solvents and detergents.

- Look for manufacturers with high standards for animal stewardship.

Tencel

Tencel (also known as Lyocell) is a man-made fiber produced from the natural cellulose found in wood pulp.

- Unlike rayon, Tencel production uses a closed-loop process that is more efficient and creates less pollution.

- Tencel has a very soft and luxurious feel and drapes nicely.

- Popular for travel because it doesn't wrinkle easily.

- Look for Tencel clothing that carries the Oeko-Tex Standard 100 certification.

- Tencel fiber is fully biodegradable.

Eco-Spotlight on: Greenloop

Looking for a one-stop shop for an eco-shopping spree? Look no further than Greenloop, an online retailer of ecofriendly clothing, shoes and accessories. Started by a woman from Portland, Oregon who wanted to do her part for the environment, Greenloop is dedicated to providing sustainable fashions made by companies committed to environmental stewardship and social responsibility. Products run the gamut from high-end to affordable, but be sure to check the virtual sale rack! www.thegreenloop.com

Bamboo

Bamboo is the fastest-growing plant in the world, and it thrives without any pesticides or fertilizers.

- It is naturally antibacterial, which helps control odors and prohibits bacteria growth.

- Bamboo fabric is extremely soft, and its natural absorbency keeps you cool and dry in hot weather.

- Chemicals used in the process of making bamboo fiber do generate pollution unless carefully controlled in a closed-loop system.

Unfortunately, it is difficult to know the origins of bamboo fiber, due to lack of transparency in the supply chain.

- High demand for bamboo has led to some exploitation and overharvesting of forestland in China.

Soybean Fiber

Soybean protein fiber is a renewable resource and a by-product from the manufacturing of tofu and soymilk.

- Often called "vegetable cashmere," soybean fiber is ultra soft and warm, which makes it perfect for babies!

- Drapes nicely and is easy to wash.

- Fabric holds up well over time.

Ingeo

Ingeo is a fiber made from corn by-products that are fermented and turned into a polymer material.

- Considered a high-performance fiber due to its strength and resilience.

- Naturally wicks moisture from the skin.

- Ingeo fiber is biodegradable and can even be composted.

- Uses GMO (genetically modified) corn.

Recycled Fleece

Recycled fleece is made from recycled plastic soda bottles.

- Not only keeps plastic bottles out of the trash heap, but reduces dependence on nonrenewable fossil fuel to produce virgin polyester.

- Recycled fleece is as soft and lightweight as conventional fleece.

Sustainable Shoes

Shoe manufacturing is notorious for using toxic dyes, glues and other nasty chemicals. Fortunately, more manufacturers are mending their ways by switching to earth-friendly materials like the following:

- Outsoles made from recycled car tires, inner tubes and rubber scraps.

- Soles and footbeds made out of natural cork.

- Uppers made from organic cotton, linen, hemp, jute and felted wool.

- Bamboo and chlorine-free wool shoe linings.

- Shoelaces made from recycled PET plastic.

- Water-based biodegradable glues.

- Leather and suede from certified sustainable sources.

Eco-Spotlight on:
Simple Shoes

Simple Shoes, the quirky, irreverent, sustainable shoe manufacturer, threw out the book on traditional shoe making and dedicated itself to making "shoes for a happy planet" instead. Using earth-friendly materials like recycled car tires, hemp, water-based glue and 100 percent postconsumer recycled paper for packaging, Simple Shoes is building sustainability into its business every step of the way. www.simpleshoes.com

Better Bags, Jewelry and Accessories

Ditch the polluting plastic purse, the cheap made-in-China accessories and the blood diamonds. Accessorize in eco-style with handbags, jewelry and other fun accessories made from recycled and planet-friendly materials.

- Handbags made from repurposed billboards, rice bags and even scraps from yoga mat production.

- Purses made from hemp and felted wool sweaters.

- Wallets made from recycled juice pouches and candy wrappers.

- Cell phone and iPod holders made from vintage neckties (see page 168 for instructions on how to make your own).

- Belts made from old rubber bicycle inner tubes.

- Earrings made from recycled glass, vintage beads and upcycled aluminum cans.

- Necklaces made from bottle caps, corks and scrap metal.

- Bracelets made from old Scrabble pieces and vintage typewriter keys.

- Hairpins made from vintage buttons.

Eco-Spotlight on:
Etsy

If you like crafty, handmade stuff, Etsy is the place for you! Etsy is a super creative, online marketplace for selling all things handmade. When you buy handmade, you are supporting artisans instead of corporations, community instead of faceless consumerism and creativity instead of mass production. Using Etsy's fabulous search engine, you can search for handmade goodies by color, location, recently listed items and, of course, the usual search terms. Many Etsy sellers use recycled and reclaimed materials in their work: www.etsy.com.

Shop Green

A lot of gorgeous jewelry and accessories are made in developing countries under fair trade conditions you can feel good about supporting. Look for a fair trade shop near you or visit www.originalgood.com.

Sensible Solutions for a Greener Wardrobe

Greening your closet is not just an excuse to run out and spend big bucks on a pair of designer organic cotton jeans or a fancy new hemp/silk-blend dress. Most people do not have the luxury of a complete closet makeover—and that isn't recommended. Follow these tips to find an earth-friendly, budget-minded balance that won't cramp your style.

Buy Less

Don't buy into the culture of disposable clothes. Make mindful, quality purchases instead.

• Choose quality over quantity.

• Purchase versatile pieces over specialty items that can only be worn with a few things.

• Resist the temptation to stock up on clothing just because it's cheap. There are environmental and social prices to pay for those $3 shirts.

• Don't tempt yourself—just stay out of the stores.

Think Outside the Mall

Traditional shopping malls and big-box stores are easy to rely on but usually don't have much in the way of sustainable options. You are much more likely to find unique, earth-friendly fashions at smaller independent stores and alternative retail outlets.

• **Local, independently owned stores.** If you are lucky enough to have a sustainable clothing store in your neck of the woods, great! Otherwise, keep your eyes peeled for a selection of ecofriendly fashion in your favorite local clothing store or other specialty stores.

- **Craft and gift shows.** These are a great way to find locally produced and often handmade clothing and accessories.

- **Green Living festivals and expos.** There are always plenty of vendors hawking their green wares at these large educational events.

- **Etsy.** A fabulous online resource for handmade fashion, Etsy has a much lighter footprint than something that came from a big-box store.

- **Online retailers.** Sometimes it's easier to shop online. Sometimes it's a necessity. Rest assured there are plenty of online resources for eco-friendly duds, bags and baubles.

Buy Used

Extend the useful life of clothing and accessories, save money and build a stylish wardrobe all at the same time. What's not to love?

- **Thrift and resale stores.** Purchase secondhand clothing and accessories at bargain-basement prices. Goods are typically donated, and condition of merchandise varies. Look for a thrift store near you at www.thethriftshopper.com.

- **Consignment stores.** These have "better" brands and higher-end fashion for a much lower price than brand new—a great way to find a variety of brands all in one place. Merchandise is typically in excellent condition, and the original owner gets a cut of the sale price. A good resource for jewelry as well.

- **eBay and craigslist.** Shop from home for pre-loved apparel. You can limit the search to your local area to avoid shipping costs.

- **Freecycle.** You might be able to get your clothes for free! Search online for a Freecycle group near you at www.freecycle.org.

Shop Green

Diane at Big Green Purse (www.biggreenpurse.com) has a smart tip for ecoshoppers: Make a line item in your budget for clothing and stick to it. It will help limit impulse buying, and when you do want to make an ecofriendly purchase, you don't have to spend a minute feeling guilty about it.

158

Adventures in Green Living

One Christmas I splurged and bought my boys organic cotton pajamas from Hanna Andersson. They are so incredibly soft, their hallmark striped fabric is so cute and I felt good about supporting a more sustainable side of the clothing industry. But like I said, it was a splurge. I can't afford to buy pricey organic clothes all the time. Truth be told, the majority of my clothing budget is spent at thrift and consignment stores.

- **Garage sales.** Great bargains can be found by perusing your local garage sales—particularly good for children's clothing and shoes!

- **Antique stores and estate sales.** These venues can be especially lucrative for finding high-quality used jewelry and vintage clothing.

- **Clothing swap parties.** Bring gently used clothes to share and go home with something new-for-you.

Clothing swaps can be highly organized affairs or simply a fun excuse for a party with friends. Either way, it's a win-win for everyone!

Repair and Refashion

Don't let a hole in the knee or a stain on the front of a shirt be a first-class ticket to the landfill.

- Fix holes with funky fabric patches or look for easy iron-on patches at your local fabric store.

159

Practically Green

Do you look at darning socks and mending holes as something no one but your grandma would do? Maybe it's time to rethink that disposable mentality. You can start by picking up a needle and thread.

- Cover up stains with fabric appliqués or fabric paint stencils.

- Breathe new life into old clothes by embellishing them with ribbon, new buttons, decorative trim or contrasting fabric.

- Turn worn or damaged items into something completely different. An old sweater becomes a set of drink coasters. Beads from a broken necklace become a new pair of earrings. A jeans pocket becomes a child's purse. You get the gist.

- See the Do It Green section for project ideas and instructions.

Pass It On

Donate or consign your old clothing, shoes and accessories for someone else to enjoy.

- **Thrift and consignment stores.** Donate used goods to a thrift store near you or make a few bucks to put toward your next clothing purchase by consigning them. Some consignment shops give you cash on the spot; others pay you a percentage of the sale price later.

- **Women's shelters.** Donations of gently used women's, children's and infant items are greatly appreciated.

- **Dress for Success.** Provide business suits, blouses, dress shoes, briefcases and other business apparel to women in need (www. dressforsuccess.org).

- **Soles4Souls.** Donate your gently worn shoes to help people around the world (www.soles4souls.org).

- **The Glass Slipper Project (Chicago area).** Pass on your almost new prom dresses and accessories to high school students who cannot afford brand new attire. For a listing

Eco-Spotlight on:
Once Upon a Child

Once Upon a Child is a retailer that sells "Kids Stuff with Previous Experience." They know that kids outgrow their stuff mighty quickly, so they provide a convenient way for parents to buy and sell gently used items. The independently owned locations around the country offer baby gear, dress shoes, winter coats and everything in between.

of similar programs in your state, visit www.glassslipperproject.org/yostate.htm.

- **Freecycle.** Give away what you don't want to someone who does.

Recycle It

Even when clothing and footwear have reached the end of their useful lives, it doesn't mean they're destined for the landfill. Send worn-out items to purposeful recycling programs or turn them into rags to use around the home.

- **Patagonia.** Send in used fleece, long underwear and Patagonia cotton T-shirts to the Common Threads Garment Recycling Program, and they will be used in the production of new garments.

- **Project Rejeaneration.** Send back your old Del Forte jeans to be regenerated into funky, new styles and you'll get 10 percent off a new pair of their organic cotton jeans.

- **Nike Reuse-A-Shoe.** Old sport shoes (any brand) are ground up and used to resurface sports fields and running tracks. Many states have drop-off collection sites (www.nikereuseashoe.com).

- **SolesUnited.** Donate worn-out Crocs to be made into new SolesUnited recycled shoes that are donated to people in need around the world (www.solesunited.com).

- **Earth911.** Check the local listings for recycling options in your area (www.earth911.com).

Even Greener

Ragstock, a pioneer in the secondhand clothing business, goes a step beyond just selling used clothing. Anything they receive that does not meet their stringent quality standards is cut up into rags instead of being sent to the landfill.

161

Do It Green

If you have even an ounce of creativity in you, you'll have loads of fun turning old clothing into new wearable fashion and other useful household accessories. Refashion clothes by adding fabric designs, decorative trim or new buttons or repurpose them into something completely different like a purse or a set of drink coasters! Start with something simple like sewing a fabric appliqué onto a T-shirt. Pretty soon you'll be itching to doctor up half the clothes in your closet. Get ready to create by keeping the following tips in mind.

- Start a box of old clothes you think you might use for future projects. This will be your inspiration box—ready for when the crafty mood strikes.

- Cull through any fabric scraps you have that might make good appliqués or trim.

- Hit the thrift stores for wool sweaters if you want to work with felt but don't have a stash of old sweaters yet.

- Keep your eyes peeled for decorative trim and vintage buttons when you're out and about.

- Keep items that simply need mending in a separate pile.

Appliqués and Embellishments

Whether you have a stained T-shirt to deal with or you just want to gussy up a pair of plain-Jane jeans, there are plenty of ways to refashion clothing into fun, original designs! The sky's the limit on this one, but here are a few ideas to get you started.

Eco-Spotlight on:
Swap-O-Rama-Rama

Swap-O-Rama-Rama, the brainchild of artist Wendy Tremayne, was designed to be an alternative to out-of-control spending on fashion. To get in to a Swap-O-Rama-Rama event, bring a bag of used clothing and a few bucks to help cover event costs. Once inside you have free rein to dive into the giant pile of clothing and grab whatever you want. The really fun part comes when you attend one of many DIY workshops run by local artisans where you can sew, embroider, bead and transform your secondhand duds into fabulous eco-fashions! Look for an event near you at www.swaporamarama.com.

- Attach fabric appliqués using HeatnBond or another iron-on adhesive. Sew around edges of appliqué pieces for extra hold.

- Sew decorative trim, fringe or ruffles around the legs of jeans or the neck, hem or sleeves of a shirt.

- Sew a new pocket in a contrasting color onto a shirt or a pair of pants.

- Trade out plain buttons for fancy ones.

- Add buttons or ribbon to decorate the front of a shirt or pant legs.

- Make new fabric cuffs for a shirt in contrasting fabric.

Rocket-T Appliqué

What little boy wouldn't love this whimsical rocket design on his T-shirt? Fabric pieces come from ripped blue jeans and old shirts or sweaters. Use this technique with the flower pattern below for an adorable fix up to a girl's shirt.

What You Need

T-shirt

Coordinating fabric

HeatnBond

Coordinating thread

How to Make It

Step 1: Cut out appliqué pieces (two patterns are provided).

Step 2: Apply HeatnBond ultrahold iron-on adhesive (following product directions) to appliqué pieces and to T-shirt.

Step 3: Sew around edges of appliqué pieces.

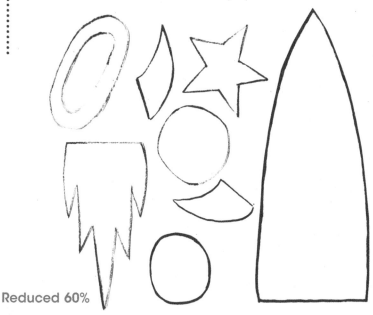

Reduced 60%

Freezer Paper Stencils

Turn a thrift store shirt into something you'd expect to find in a high-end boutique. All you need is freezer paper, fabric paint and a little imagination! Use the bus pattern or make up your own.

What You Need

T-shirt

Freezer paper (unlike waxed paper, freezer paper is waxed on only one side)

Tape

Craft knife

Heavy-duty mat

Iron

Nontoxic fabric paint

Paintbrush

How to Make It

Step 1: Place freezer paper (waxed-side down), on top of pattern. Tape down to stabilize.

Step 2: Cut out stencil using the craft knife. (Be sure to put a heavy-duty mat underneath your cutting surface.)

Step 3: Iron the freezer paper stencil onto shirt, with the waxed side down.

Step 4: Paint inside the stencil. **Note:** Before painting, place a piece of cardboard or another piece of freezer paper between the front of the shirt and the back to prevent paint from leaking through.

Step 5: After paint has dried for 24 hours (follow paint manufacturer's directions), carefully remove freezer paper. Iron shirt on reverse side to heat set the paint. Wait at least 3 days before washing the garment.

Reduced 50%

166

Stretchy Baby Bunny Hat

Turn a favorite old stretchy T-shirt into an adorable baby hat with bunny ears.

What You Need

Stretchy T-shirt
(ribbed cotton
works best)

Coordinating thread

Coordinating ribbon

Adventures in Green Living

One of my favorite T-shirts was ruined when a couple of crayons went through the washer and dryer cycles. I was really bummed! Instead of tossing it straight into the trash, I kept it in my project pile and eventually used the fabric for a baby bunny hat!

How to Make It

Step 1: Turn T-shirt inside out. Pin hat pattern onto shirt, using side seam as one of the edges.

Step 2: Cut out pattern, leaving side seam intact where possible.

Step 3: Sew seams using $1/2$" (1cm) seam allowance.

Step 4: Turn hat right-side out. Push ears out with the eraser end of a pencil.

Step 5: Tie bows onto ears with ribbon.

Reduced 75%

167

Necktie Bag

This is a great project for those long-forgotten neckties lying around your house or for the super cool vintage one you found at the thrift store. With a quick flip and a couple side seams (well, it's almost that easy), a tie becomes a nifty little bag for your cell phone, sunglasses or iPod.

What You Need

Necktie

Coordinating thread

Velcro closure

Decorative cord
for strap

How to Make It

Step 1: Cut necktie at 13" (33cm) from the wide end of the tie.

Step 2: Fold edge under $\frac{1}{4}$" (6mm) and then another $\frac{3}{4}$" (19cm). Press and pin to secure. Hand-sew the bottom edge closed. This will create the channel for the strap.

Step 3: Open up a few inches of the center seam of the tie. This will make it easier to fit things inside the case.

Step 4: Fold the tie in half (wrong sides together) so the bottom edge reaches just below where the tie becomes a triangle. Using a slipstitch, hand sew the side seams through the top layers of fabric. Do not sew the front and back of the case together, or you will not be able to put anything inside!

Step 5: Add a Velcro closure (follow manufacturer's directions).

Step 6: Thread cord through channel. Cut to desired length and sew together or secure with a knot. Hand sew the cord in place.

168

Felted Sweater Mittens

You'll be warm and ecostylish this winter when you wear these adorable mittens made from felted wool sweaters. Use cashmere for super soft mittens or a thick wool sweater for extra warmth.

What You Need

Felted sweater with ribbing at the hem (this becomes the mitten cuffs)

Contrasting felted sweater for star appliqué

Coordinating thread

How to Make It

Step 1: Trace around your hand on a sheet of paper, including extra for cuff.

Step 2: Add $\frac{1}{2}$" (1cm) around for seam allowance

Step 3: Pin pattern onto the sweater next to the side seam.

Step 4: Cut out mitten through both sides of the sweater.

Step 5: Cut out star appliqué, using pattern below. Hand sew onto the top side of each mitten.

Step 6: Pin right sides together and machine sew. (If wool is too thick, you may have to hand sew.) Trim seam allowances.

Step 7: Turn mitten right-side out. Repeat with other mitten.

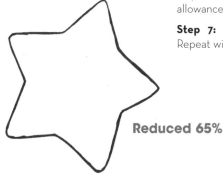

Reduced 65%

Chapter 6: Conserving

Chapter 6: Conserving
Less is More

Most people I know (myself included) have grown up in a culture of abundance. We have all the food we can possibly eat, all the water we care to pour, all the heat we need to stay toasty warm—all within arms' reach and at a reasonable cost. We are incredibly lucky, but the downside is that we tend to be wasteful. We leave the water running when we brush our teeth. We throw perfectly good food in the garbage. We buy clothing we don't need. Our culture of abundance has turned into a culture of excess. And this culture of excess is bad for the planet.

These days, terms like *global warming, climate change* and *carbon footprint* (your carbon footprint is the total amount of greenhouse gas emissions caused directly by you) are commonplace—and that should make us worried. Runaway consumerism and an attitude of entitlement has led us to this point. Perhaps it's time to reexamine our lives and look for ways to conserve the resources we are so lucky to have rather than waste them.

That said, I'm trying hard to be a more mindful consumer of resources these days. That means thinking twice about whether I really need something before I buy it and often passing up on the "good deals" that come my way. It means actively buying products that generate less waste and figuring out how to recycle much more than aluminum cans. It means keeping a closer eye on my consumption of resources like energy and water in my home. It also means being creative and resourceful by finding new ways to use things and learning how to get by with less.

In many ways I have found that less is more. My kitchen looks much better with fewer appliances on the counter than it does cluttered up with all the latest gadgets. It's easier for my son to pick out an outfit to wear when there are fewer clothes in his drawer to choose from. It costs less, too: When I buy in bulk instead of buying excessively packaged products or lower my energy bills by making environmentally friendly changes to my home, I have more money in the bank for other things.

In this chapter you will discover how easy it is to conserve resources in your home. Not only are most of the ideas pretty painless, but they will often save you money. The Buy It Green section is filled with practical advice and guidelines for reducing the amount of stuff you buy and cutting way back on the amount of waste you bring to the curb. It also contains tips for managing energy and water consumption in your home in ways that may surprise you.

In the Do It Green section of this chapter, I'm hoping to help you get up and over any hurdles you may have about taking action to conserve resources and to show you how to make the most of what you already have. I'll also share my secrets for how to throw a green birthday party and give you the scoop on a couple practical ecocrafts. After reading this chapter, I hope you will find that consuming less can truly give you more!

Buy It Green

Next time you head to the store, find a way to rebel against the culture of excess and its negative impact on the environment. You have more power than you think—the power to shift your spending to products with greater environmental benefit, the power to reduce the amount of waste you produce, the power to cut back on resources used in your home and the power to choose not to buy something. It all counts!

Control Consumption

Don't let rampant consumerism get a hold of your life. Follow these guidelines for making smart and sustainable purchase decisions based on conserving resources in as many ways as possible.

Buy Less

Before you put that item into your cart, before you step into the checkout line, before you click the *accept* button for an Internet order, ask yourself these questions:

- Do I really need it?

- Do I already have something that can do the job just as well?

- Can I wait and see if I really want it later?

If you ask yourself these questions, I bet you'll find you don't need to make the purchase at least 20 percent of the time. Try it and see!

Buy Mindfully

Try to avoid those mindless trips to the shopping mall. Instead, plan shopping trips ahead of time and give careful thought to how you choose to spend your money.

Buy Locally

Skip the big-box store and head to a local small business or craftsperson to find what you are looking for.

- Locally produced goods use less energy for transportation.

- For every $100 spent at a locally owned business, approximately $45 goes back into the community. That strengthens the local economy.

- Check your local phone book, area events guides or neighborhood newspapers for small businesses near you.

- Don't forget: The "buy local" mantra is not just for food but for durable goods as well.

Buy Used

Before you head to the mall, consider buying something that has been gently used instead. You will almost certainly pay less, and you'll be keeping a perfectly good product out of the landfill. There is no shortage of resources for used products:

- **Thrift and secondhand stores.** Great for clothing, kitchen accessories, home decor and even furniture. If you like treasure hunts, you'll love shopping thrift!

- **Yard and estate sales.** Whether you just drop by a neighborhood sale or spend the day sale-hopping, you are bound to find something interesting. Most are cash-and-carry. If you don't know where to begin, check your local newspaper's classified section for garage sale listings.

- **Classified sales or auction Web sites.** Hop online and see what you can find. These Internet-based

Shop Green

Warehouse club stores like Costco and Sam's Club can be a great way to save money. But beware the temptation to buy large quantities of junk food or more food than you can realistically eat. Stop and think before you buy: Do you really need a five- pound bag of M&M's? Will you use up a three-liter bottle of olive oil before it goes bad? Is having a five-year supply of Post-it notes at home really a good thing?

Mindful Shopping Techniques

Mindful shopping can't be turned on like a light switch—it takes practice. From choosing the most ecofriendly items to not buying them at all, mindful shopping is a way to consider all your options. Here are some examples.

What to Do	How to Do It
Buy fewer-high quality items	• Buy a set of durable, glass food storage containers instead of cheap plastic ones that will need to be replaced frequently • Get a pair of sturdy jeans for your child instead of trendy, inexpensive pants that will wear through at the knees
Look for multipurpose products rather than specialized products	• Use an ecofriendly, all-purpose household cleaner rather than separate sprays for kitchen, bathroom and disinfecting • Use a combination moisturizer and foundation or a lip balm with color instead of separate cosmetics for every application
Focus on experiences rather than stuff	• Give a gift of theater tickets rather than a new set of knickknacks • Make a batch of homemade cookies with your kids instead of buying pricey store-bought treats
Don't buy it just because it's cheap	• Your favorite store might be having a sale, but don't buy more than you can reasonably use • Keep in mind that cheap prices often mean cheap quality • Food waste is the largest contributor to global warming in the landfill. Limit purchases to what you know you can eat
Skip the window shopping	• If temptation is your middle name, just stay away from it • That includes Internet shopping!

sites are great when you are looking for something specific. But be prepared to act quickly when you do find something special—good things go fast! Limit the search to your local area if you want to avoid shipping costs: www.craigslist.org, www.ebay.com.

• **Swap sites.** Trade what you no longer need for something you do need. Most swap sites operate on a point-based system as opposed to an item-for-item exchange, and shipping fees are the only cost. Popular sites for books, CDs, DVDs, video games, clothing and baby equipment:

Eco-Spotlight on:
The Compact

Have you heard of the Compact? Started by a small group of friends in San Francisco who wanted to get off the consumer grid, the Compact is essentially a pledge not to buy anything new (except essentials like food and toilet paper) for a year at a time. The group has blossomed into a fairly large community committed to swapping, bartering, thrifting, freecycling and even dumpster diving to get what they need. To get connected with other people who are committed to the Compact, check out the Yahoo group at http://groups.yahoo.com/group/thecompact.

www.swaptree.com, www.bookmooch.com, www.swapstyle.com, www.zwaggle.com.

• **Freebie Web sites.** As the popular saying goes, "One person's trash is another person's treasure." From silverware to computers to children's play equipment—even houseplants—you will be amazed at what you can get for free: www.freecycle.org, www.freesharing.org, www.freeuse.org.

Rent or Borrow

Why buy when you can borrow? Save money and keep the clutter out of your house by taking advantage of the many options for renting and borrowing common household items.

• **Libraries.** Pick up a new stash of books to read to your kids every week or put a hold on that hot new best seller. It's all free at your local library!

• **Video rentals.** Unless it's a classic you'll watch over and over again, it seems like a waste to purchase videos that will collect dust on the shelf. Head to your local video store or use Netflix or a similar program to keep a standing order for exactly what you want to see.

- **Tool-lending libraries.** Consider yourself lucky if your community offers this very valuable resource for borrowing tools. You can find tools for a variety of purposes including carpentry, plumbing, electrical work and gardening—all for free!

- **Toy-lending programs.** This is a great way to keep your kids entertained without spending a fortune on toys. Children can borrow a toy for a week or two at a time and then switch it for something new. Typically offered through community organizations or early childhood educational programs.

- **Car-sharing programs.** Why pay to maintain and insure a car if you really don't use it much? Car-sharing programs offer the convenience of a car whenever you need it in return for a small monthly membership fee and an hourly rental charge.

- **Neighbors.** One of your most valuable resources may be right next door. Having a give-and-take relationship with your neighbors is good for community building and is easier on the pocketbook.

- **Web-based borrowing groups.** These Web sites facilitate the lending of tools, toys, books and other household items within a community. Start a group in your community: www.borrowingcircle.com, www.neighborrow.com.

Adventures in Green Living

My husband and I own an old house that was remodeled in the 1970s (think jungle wallpaper and purple shag carpet). Slowly but surely we have been trying to return the house back to its late-1800s splendor. Imagine how thrilled we were when we found an oak mantelpiece on eBay that matched the woodwork in our home perfectly! It felt great to reuse something from another old house and bring it back to life in our own way.

Reuse

Think twice before you head to the store—you may have something in your home already that can do the job!

What You Need	What You Already Have
A jar to store nuts, rolled oats or other grains purchased in bulk	Glass jars from spaghetti sauce or applesauce
A container to hold children's art supplies like paintbrushes or crayons	Plastic yogurt tubs, empty wipes containers or plastic drink cups kids often get from restaurants
A place to sort beads or buttons	Egg cartons
Rags to clean up spills around the house	Old T-shirts and socks
Drawer organizers for socks or office supplies	Shoe boxes, personal check boxes or any small cardboard box
Plant starters	Cardboard egg cartons (when it's time to plant, place the cup right in the ground—it will disintegrate)
Trash bags	Plastic shopping bags

Adventures in Green Living

A couple years ago, my husband and I made the commitment to have only one car. My husband rides his bike to work, and our second car was sitting idle most of the time. When we first embarked on this adventure we thought we might need to use a car-sharing program (Hourcar is the business in our area) every once in a while for short trips around town. It turns out that we haven't needed it. It's pretty easy to plan our schedules around our one car, and only rarely do we rent a car for special events.

Reduce Waste

Limit the amount of garbage you kick to the curb by purchasing goods with waste reduction in mind. You may even be able to lower your garbage collection fees by switching to monthly instead of biweekly pick-up. Challenge yourself to see how low you can go!

Limit Packaging

According to the Environmental Protection Agency (EPA), nearly 80 million tons of waste from packaging and containers make their way to landfills each year. You can greatly reduce the amount of packaging waste in your garbage can by simply not bringing it home in the first place.

Instead of	Buy
Precut fruits and vegetables in plastic containers	Whole fruits and vegetables
Regular laundry detergent and dish soap	Concentrated versions of the same products
Individually packaged applesauce	Large container of applesauce
Toys packaged in plastic clamshells (that are impossible to open)	Toys sold with minimal packaging
Small bottles of body care products	Buy the largest size that makes sense for your family
Individually packaged chocolates	A large bar of chocolate that can be split into smaller pieces
Meat packaged in nonrecyclable Styrofoam trays	Meat wrapped in butcher paper at the counter

Even Greener

Take this philosophy with you when you go out to eat as well. Order ice cream in a cone instead of a plastic dish. Skip the plastic lid and straw when you get a drink. Some people I know even carry reusable utensils in their purse so they don't need to waste the disposable kind.

Eco-Spotlight on: Frustration-Free Packaging

Amazon.com now offers a selection of products with "frustration-free packaging." Instead of hard plastic clamshells, plastic bindings and wire ties, products come packaged in a simple recyclable cardboard box. Not only will it save you from "wrap rage," it is much easier on the environment.

Practically Green

With two growing boys and an active husband, we go through a lot of oatmeal. To save time, I got into the habit of buying individual oatmeal packets. But when I thought about the environmental impact of all those little packages, I changed my tune and started buying large containers of dried oats instead. Taking it one step further, I began to refill my large container with oats from the bulk bins at my local co-op. This little change in habit is not only much better for environment, it also saves me money.

Refill, Refill, Refill

Refilling product containers is one of the most impactful ways to reduce packaging waste in the home. You may be surprised to learn how many different types of products can be refilled. A food co-op or health food store will offer the largest selection of bulk products, but even conventional grocery stores are getting in on the act.

Words to the wise: If you bring an empty container to the store, be sure to weigh it before you fill it so you won't get charged for the weight of the container at checkout. Just write down the container weight (called the tare weight) and the bin number (sometimes called a PLU or price lookup number) on the label or twist tie. It's easy!

Be Selective

Just a quick word about free stuff: Don't take if you're not going to use it.

Aim for One Can a Month

By following the simple steps in this section, you can greatly reduce the amount of garbage your household produces.

- Check with your municipal waste management office to see if you can switch to a monthly garbage pickup or a smaller garbage can. The savings should be reflected in your monthly waste utility bill. An added bonus: You'll save money on garbage bags.

- For even further waste reduction, try composting your food waste (see page 198).

Adventures in Green Living

I have to admit that buying products in bulk was a little intimidating when I was first starting out. I wasn't exactly sure what to do. Could I bring a container from home? Did I need to weigh it myself? What if I made a big mess? I was afraid I would do something wrong and be totally embarrassed. Asking for help was the key to overcoming my fear, and it's been smooth sailing (or should I say filling?) ever since.

Bulk Buying 101

Category	Types of Products	How-To
Dry foods	Nuts, grains, seeds, beans, flour and other baking products, pasta, granola and other cereals, dried fruits, spices, coffee and tea, snacks	• Bring jars or bags from home and fill them up with whatever you need • Reusable cotton food bags are a nice investment • Stores have plastic bags available if you forget your own
Wet, liquid and refrigerated foods	Peanut and other nut butters, cooking oils, vinegar, soy sauce, sweeteners like honey, maple syrup and agave nectar, pine nuts, flaxseed and brewer's yeast	• Fill up your own container to avoid having to purchase a new one • Save original containers from products like peanut butter or honey • Plastic containers are usually available for purchase
Dairy products	Milk, cream and eggs	• Pay a deposit on a glass milk or cream bottle. Then bring it back to the store for credit and pick up a fresh bottle • Bring an egg carton from home to pack your own fresh eggs
Personal care products	Shampoo, conditioner, body lotion, styling products, bubble bath, massage oil, etc.	• Bring an empty bottle from home and refill it from the selection of bulk products available
Cleaning products	Dishwashing liquid, laundry detergent, all-purpose cleaner, glass cleaner, etc.	• Fill up your original bottle at an in-store refill station or with a refill pouch
Printer cartridges	Many brands for home office printers	• Bring in used printer cartridges to be refilled at your local office supply store or refill kiosk

Buy Reusable, Not Disposable

Disposable products sure are convenient, but there is a big environmental price to pay for all the garbage they create. Investing in reusable products may require a higher initial cost, but they almost always save you money in the long run.

Instead of	Buy
Paper towels and disposable wipes	• Cotton washcloths for wiping kids' messy faces • Reusable microfiber cloths for dusting and polishing • Keep a supply of absorbent cotton rags or cloths under the sink for cleaning up messes
Disposable plates, cups and utensils	• Reusable tableware made from recycled plastic • Plates and utensils made from ecofriendly bamboo (bambu is a popular brand)
Disposable batteries	• Rechargeable batteries
Disposable razors	• Reusable razors • Better yet, buy a razor made from recycled plastic like those from Preserve
Swiffer and similar disposable cleaning cloths for sweeping and mopping	• Durable, reusable cleaning tools • Method's omop uses washable microfiber mop pads
Disposable cameras	• Invest in an inexpensive digital camera
Facial tissues	• Reusable handkerchiefs are making a big comeback

Be Prepared

"Be prepared" isn't just a Boy Scout motto, it's the cry of the ecoconcious. Stowing durable, reusable items in strategic places can keep you from adding to the landfill.

Having	Keeps You From Wasting
A reusable water bottle with you at all times	Disposable plastic water bottles purchased spur of the moment
A reusable coffee mug in your bag	Paper cups at the coffee shop or office
Reusable grocery bags in the car	Plastic or paper bags at the grocery store
A compact bag (like a ChicoBag) in your purse	A plastic bag at the gift shop (skip the bag completely for small purchases you can carry)
Reusable utensils at your desk	Plastic utensils from the takeout place

 Even Greener

Go one step further by purchasing products with packaging made from recycled materials. Look for the universal recycling symbol on the back or bottom of a package, accompanied by language indicating the percentage of recycled content as well as the percentage (if any) of postconsumer waste used. (Postconsumer waste is material that has previously been used by consumers, as opposed to factory scraps that were never part of a product to begin with.) Products that may come in recycled packaging include:

- Packaged foods like cereal and cookies in recycled paperboard boxes.
- Shampoo and other personal care products in bottles made with recycled plastic.
- Household cleaning products packaged in recycled plastic bottles.
- Toothpaste tubes made with recycled metal.

Practically Green

According to the US Department of Energy, heating and cooling accounts for over half the total energy used in an average home. In colder climates (like Minnesota, where I live), heating alone can make up two-thirds of the bill. A rule of thumb is that you will save 1 to 2 percent on your heating bill for every one degree you lower the thermostat.

Manage Home Energy Use

Energy usage is a major factor when it comes to conserving resources in the home. Fortunately, there are many ways you can boost energy efficiency without sacrificing comfort. Begin with the tips that don't cost anything (a change in habit is all that is required), and then pick out some low-cost ideas. Finally, consider making energy-saving investments in your home that will save you money in the long run. Remember, every little step makes a difference.

No Cost

Let's start with the freebies: You don't have to pay a dime to make these simple changes that can save you a real chunk of change over the course of a year.

- Turn down the heat and put on a sweater. Lowering the temperature by even one degree makes a difference for the planet and in your wallet.

- Don't overuse air conditioning. It doesn't need to feel like a deep freezer in order to be a refreshing change from the summer heat.

- Close off rooms that are rarely used either by shutting the door or closing the air vent in the room.

- Keep blinds or drapes open on sunny winter days to take advantage of the sun's heat. Keep them closed on hot summer days to keep heat out.

- Turn off the lights when you leave the room, especially if you are using incandescent light bulbs. Fluorescent light bulbs should be turned off when you leave a room for fifteen minutes or more.

- Unplug cell phone chargers and any appliances or electronics that are not frequently used. This small step can save you up to 10 percent on your energy bill.

- Set your computer to hibernate or sleep mode to reduce energy use during the day.

- Turn the hot water heater down to 120 degrees. You probably won't even notice the difference (except in your energy bill).

- Wash clothes in cold water. Cold cleans just as well as warm and could save you $60 or more per year.

- Clean the lint screen in your clothes dryer after every use. It will run more efficiently, and you'll save a bit on your electricity bill.

- Better yet, skip the dryer and air-dry clothing outside.

- Clean exposed coils on your refrigerator to keep it running efficiently.

- Close the fireplace damper when it is not in use to stop air from escaping up the flue.

- Complete a free, do-it-yourself home energy audit online at http://hes.lbl.gov to find out what else you can do to make your home more energy efficient.

Low Cost

These minimal investments will buy you supplies and services that will most certainly make a dent in your annual home energy bills.

- Change the filters on heating and air conditioning units at least once a month during peak usage times.

- Caulk and weather strip around windows and doors to help stop air drafts.

- Cover windows with plastic film to reduce heat loss.

- Purchase insulated window blinds or curtains to keep heat inside.

- Install a programmable thermostat that adjusts your furnace to lower temperatures while you are sleeping or away from home. As little as $25 buys a basic model. Pay a bit more for increased programming abilities.

- Arrange for a professional home energy audit to get specific recommendations for improving the energy efficiency of your home. Contact your local utility provider to find out if they offer this service or look for a certified home energy rater at www.resnet.us. A thorough audit will include a blower-door test to measure airflow and infrared cameras to help pinpoint leaks.

- Use power strips to turn off appliances and electronics when they are not in use, which stops the unnecessary energy drain that happens even when appliances are off.

- Give your hot water heater a little love by wrapping it in an insulated blanket to help stop heat loss.

- Make the switch to compact fluorescent (CFL) and light-emitting diode (LED) light bulbs. The initial cost is higher than incandescent, but lower energy use saves you money over the life of the bulb.

- Get rid of the gas mower and buy a push mower instead—you'll get your

Even Greener

Ditch your conventional wall adapter for a charging device that gets its energy from the sun. Solar-powered chargers are perfect for people on the go, but there's no reason why you can't use them at home as well.

exercise and knock a chore off the list at the same time.

- Purchase renewable energy through your local utility. It may cost a bit more, but you'll feel good about supporting a worthy, environmental cause!

Energy-Saving Investments

For a little more dough, you can make changes that will have a big impact on your environmental footprint and will definitely save you money in the long run.

- Replace leaky, old windows with high-efficiency storm windows.

- Invest in new insulation for your home. The attic is usually the best place to start.

- Purchase an energy-efficient furnace when it's time to replace your old one.

- Upgrade appliances to energy-efficient models when they are at the end of their useful life. Energy Star–qualified models use considerably less energy than conventional models. For energy-saving comparisons see www.energystar.gov.

Conserve Water

We have a tendency to think that water is free and everlasting because of the ease in which it flows from our taps. The truth is, only about 1 percent of Earth's water is drinkable. To make matters worse, the drinking water that is pumped into our homes is also used to wash dishes, water lawns and bathe our bodies. Personal water use varies greatly per person, but the average American drains at least one hundred gallons of water per day. Lower your daily drain by following these tips.

Pay Attention

- **Take a shorter shower.** You'll save about ten gallons of water for every two minutes you cut from your shower time.

- **Turn off the water when brushing your teeth.** The average tap runs at two to four gallons per minute.

- **Fix leaks and drips ASAP.** Dripping faucets can waste up to two thousand gallons of water each year.

- **Scrape your dishes.** Don't prerinse your dishes before you put them in the dishwasher; this unnecessary step wastes about 6,500 gallons of water a year.

- **Water the lawn at the right times.** It's best to water the lawn in the early morning or in the evening when heat evaporation is at its lowest point.

Go Low-Flow and High-Tech

- **Install a low-flow showerhead.** It can lower water consumption by five hundred gallons or more per month and reduce hot water use by up to 50 percent.

- **Pop a faucet aerator onto your sink fixture.** This is a really cheap way to reduce water flow by 40 to 50 percent.

- **Invest in a low-flow toilet.** You will cut out two to five gallons per flush. You can create your own low-flow system by putting a full plastic bottle in the tank to displace water and lower the amount used per flush.

- **Use soaker hoses in the garden.** These highly efficient hoses use up to 70 percent less water than conventional sprinklers.

- **Switch to a tankless hot water heater.** These on-demand water heaters eliminate the need to run water until it gets hot.

- **Invest in a front-loading washing machine.** Energy Star–qualified models can save up to seven thousand gallons of water a year.

Use What Nature Provides

- **Install a rain barrel to collect water from your home's gutters.** Rain barrels are available at many gardening and home improvement stores or, if you're lucky, at reduced rates through a city program or community environmental group. Use the spigot at the bottom of the barrel to fill watering cans or attach a hose.

- **Don't overwater your garden.** Rely on Mother Nature as much as possible and supplement with a hose only when truly needed.

Adventures in Green Living

Our high-efficiency furnace drains condensed water (a product of the heating process) into the sink in our laundry room. Instead of letting that perfectly good grey water go down the drain, I collect it in a watering can and use it on my houseplants. Admittedly, I sometimes feel like a crazy lady for all the little eco-minded things I do around the house, but each one is an important way to save our precious natural resources!

Do It Green

Spending green is certainly not the only way to be a part of the environmental movement. There are countless ways to care for the planet without spending a dime. What it will take is a commitment to spending your own time and energy on activities that make better use of the resources you have. Be warned: You may have to change some well-established habits. Once you start, though, you'll wonder how you ever did it any other way.

Commit to Recycling

Recycling is one of the biggest trends to hit the planet, but you may be surprised to know that up to 75 percent of what Americans throw in the garbage could actually be recycled. That's a lot of useful stuff going to the dump. The benefits of recycling go well beyond simply reducing the need for landfill space. Recycling also:

- **Protects nature.** It uses fewer natural resources.

- **Helps prevent global warming.** It limits the release of greenhouse gases into the air. Landfills are notorious producers of methane, a potent greenhouse gas.

- **Saves energy and lessens pollution.** It creates products with previously used materials instead of brand new raw materials.

- **Creates jobs.** Imagine ten thousand tons of waste. Incinerating it creates one job and landfilling it creates six jobs, while recycling it creates thirty-six jobs.

- **Saves money.** Well-designed recycling programs cost less to operate than waste collection, landfilling and incineration.

So are you ready to get on board to become a better recycler? Follow this easy three-step program to get on track to recycle everything you possibly can.

Eco-Alert:

Can you imagine throwing out one in every four beer bottles and almost all your plastic containers instead of recycling them? If you did, you would be keeping up with the Joneses. According to the EPA, less than 25 percent of glass waste and less than 10 percent of plastic waste generated is currently recycled. Here's a case where keeping up with the Joneses is a bad idea.

Step 1: Get to know your curbside recycling program.

Not everyone is lucky enough to have a curbside recycling program, but if you have one, it is important to understand what it takes, and even more importantly, what it doesn't take. Curbside recycling programs are different in every community, but a typical program includes the following types of materials:

• Glass bottles and containers.

• Metal cans (aluminum and steel).

• Plastic bottles with recycling codes #1 and #2.

• Newspaper, mixed paper and cardboard.

Some curbside programs require participants to sort and separate materials by type; others allow all materials to be collected in one bin. Be sure you know the rules for your particular program.

It's worth mentioning a few things that you should definitely *not* pop into the recycling bin:

• **Pizza boxes.** The oil from pizza penetrates the cardboard, making it impossible to process it into new, clean paper products.

• **Napkins and paper towels.** Anything that has been used to wipe up food spills, dirt or cleaning products is considered contaminated and is no longer recyclable. That goes for wet paper, too.

• **Egg cartons.** The likelihood of the cardboard being contaminated is so high that there is no market for it. It might make you feel better to know that most cardboard egg cartons are already produced from recycled material. What about Styrofoam egg cartons? Avoid these nonrecyclable cartons or find a way to reuse them.

- **Juice boxes, milk cartons and frozen food boxes.** The paper in these types of cartons is blended with wax or other materials and cannot be separated to be recycled.

- **Plastic caps.** While most plastic bottles can be recycled, there is little market for bottle caps. Aveda is one company that has created a market for them by turning used plastic caps into new bottle caps for the Aveda line of personal care products.

Adventures in Green Living

When I first began to recycle, I was a bit overzealous in my efforts and put all the papery products I could think of into my recycling bin. I knew that pizza boxes weren't accepted, but I mistakenly included frozen food boxes and cardboard egg cartons into the mix. I never got a nasty note or anything (I've heard that happens in some communities), but I was a bit embarrassed for clogging up the recycling stream with things that can't be used.

Step 2: Get organized.

Getting organized for recycling is half the battle. If you have the space, set up a recycling station in your kitchen or pantry. Keeping separate bins for each type of material makes it easier to deal with on recycling day. Otherwise, keep smaller recycling containers around the house wherever they work for you.

Aesthetics is not a necessary requirement when collecting recyclables. Throw them in paper bags, pile them in old boxes or stack and tie them with string. However, if you prefer to keep things looking a little more polished, there are plenty of recycling bins and accessories available for purchase.

Even Greener

If you're really lucky, you live in a community that offers an expanded curbside program that includes compostable materials. These may include:

- Food scraps
- Yard waste
- Houseplant and flower trimmings
- Pizza boxes
- Cardboard egg cartons
- Milk cartons and juice containers
- Wet and soiled paper products
- Waxed paper
- Ashes from your grill
- Certified compostable utensils, cups and plates
- Coffee filters and tea bags
- Dryer lint

193

Practically Green

• Recycling one aluminum can saves enough energy to run a computer for three hours.

• It takes about five PET plastic bottles to create enough fiberfill to stuff a ski jacket.

• Every day Americans use enough steel and tin cans to make a pipe running from Los Angeles to New York and back.

• For every ton of paper recycled, seventeen trees are saved.

• **Stacking bins.** Get one each for glass, plastic and metal.

• **Sectioned organizers.** These are typically available in two- or three-section units.

• **Pull-out recycling baskets.** These fit conveniently under the kitchen counter.

• **Newspaper stacker.** This neatly organizes papers for easy bundling.

• **Plastic bag dispenser.** This keeps bags handy for reuse or recycling (see page 204 for directions on how to make your own).

Step 3: Find out where to recycle the rest.

There's a lot more to recycling than curbside pick-up programs, but knowing where to bring other recyclable items can be a hurdle. Fortunately, Earth911 is there to help. Earth911 (http://earth911.com) is a Web site that consolidates recycling resources from all across the United States. Type in your zip code and the name of the item you are looking to recycle. Earth911 then generates a list of

Adventures in Green Living

We don't have a pantry, a mudroom or any extra space at all to set up an elaborate recycling station. Instead we keep recycling bins in various places around the house. Most things go in an old wine box hidden behind the trash can in my kitchen. We also have an old yogurt tub in the closet to collect batteries and a wicker basket for paper in the office. That's what works for us.

specific recycling locations for that product in your area. Remember to always call ahead and confirm that the site is in fact taking the items for recycling. Some of the most common types of recycling locations include the following:

- **Municipal household hazardous waste disposal stations.** You may need to make an appointment or obtain a voucher to drop off materials at these sites.

- **Thrift or resale shops.** Some locations such as Goodwill Industries contract with other organizations to assure responsible recycling of computers and other electronics, as well as with rag manufacturers to recycle worn clothing.

- **Retail stores.** Home improvement, office supply or grocery stores often offer recycling of items related to products they sell in their stores. Some even hold special recycling events.

- **Buy-back centers.** These will pay cash for aluminum, glass and some plastics.

- **Drop-off recycling centers.** These are often intended for use by busi-

nesses but can be used by individuals as well. Fees may apply.

- **Recycling fundraising programs.** Recycle your cell phone, printer cartridge or other small electronics and raise money for your school or other community organizations. Cartridges for Kids (www.cartridgesforkids. com) is one such organization.

Practically Green

Recycling efforts in the United States provide an annual benefit of reducing carbon emissions by almost fifty million metric tons. That's comparable to removing almost forty million passenger cars from the road each year.

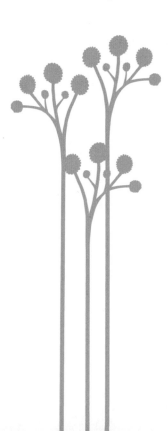

195

(a copy-and-clip guide)

Where Can I Recycle That?

There are some items people never think to recycle, either because the items are disposed of infrequently or they just seem too odd a candidate for the bin. Keep this handy guide next to a recycling bin marked *other* to know what you can recycle and where.

Item	Where to Recycle
Appliances	• Many appliance and home improvement stores will take back your old appliance when you buy a new one • Drop-off centers • For refrigerators, check www.energystar.gov/recycle
Car batteries	• Household hazardous waste disposal locations
Carpet	• Household hazardous waste disposal locations • Drop-off centers • Carpet America Recovery Effort (www.carpetrecovery.org) has a list of locations that accept carpet for recycling
Cell phones	• Household hazardous waste disposal locations • FedEx Office drop-off boxes • Staples and other office store locations • Charitable organizations such as www.collectivegood.com and www.charitablerecycling.com • Fundraising programs
CFL light bulbs	• Household hazardous waste disposal locations • Home Depot and some hardware stores
Cleaning products and other household chemicals	• Household hazardous waste disposal locations
Clothes hangers and dry cleaner bags	• Dry cleaners
Computers and other electronics	• Some Goodwill locations • Manufacturer- or retailer-sponsored recycling events • Drop-off centers and recovery programs that specialize in electronics recycling (fees may apply) • Staples and Office Depot (fees may apply) • Fundraising programs

(a copy-and-clip guide)

Item	Where to Recycle
Drink pouches and snack wrappers	• Fundraising programs like www.terracycle.net
Mattresses	• Household hazardous waste disposal locations • Drop-off centers • www.emattress.com will take back mattresses purchased from them and recycle free of charge
Medicine	• Household hazardous waste disposal locations • Some pharmacies and hospitals
Packing peanuts	• Packing and shipping stores such as The UPS Store and Mail Boxes Etc. • Check online at the Alliance of Foam Packaging Recyclers (www.epspackaging.org) or the Plastic Loose Fill Council (www.loosefillpackaging.com) for a list of drop-off and mail-back locations
Paint and paint thinners	• Household hazardous waste disposal locations
Phone books	• Many curbside recycling programs
Plastic bags	• Many grocery store chains have a drop-off bin • Wal-Mart stores
Plastic containers with recycling codes #4, #5 and #6	• Some curbside programs • Special recycling events • Fundraising programs like www.terracycle.net
Printer cartridges	• Office supply stores • Fundraising programs like www.cartridgesforkids.com
Single-use batteries	• Some curbside programs • Household hazardous waste disposal locations

Practically Green

If turning a compost pile is not your style, make worms do the work instead. Vermiculture composting (also known as vermicomposting) creates super-rich compost from kitchen scraps with very little human effort. Contrary to popular belief, worm bins do not smell and are super easy to maintain. For more information, go to www.wormcompostingtips.com

Start Composting

When you toss food scraps and yard waste into the garbage can, you are throwing away precious materials that could help your plants grow tall and your garden flourish. By converting those organic materials into compost instead, you create a nutrient-rich soil and reduce your household waste by as much as 25 percent. Home composting not only provides you with free soil that acts as a natural alternative to fertilizer, but you save money on plastic leaf bags and possibly even garbage pick-up fees. If you're worried that backyard composting is too much work, read on to see how simple it can really be.

The Setup

Make or buy a compost bin for your yard. You can use something as simple as chicken wire or create a wooden bin from old scrap wood. It needn't be fancy—it's just for dirt, right? If you'd rather buy a bin there are many options, ranging from an inexpensive hoop bin made from recycled plastic to an aesthetically pleasing bin made of natural cedar.

If you don't have enough space for a bin or prefer not to have your compost out in the open, you can opt for a completely contained compost

tumbler instead. No outdoor space at all? Not to worry! You can create compost indoors in a small composter that ferments kitchen scraps.

The Recipe

The basic recipe for compost is simple and very flexible.

- **2-3 parts Browns (or dry ingredients).** Examples are dried leaves, twigs, dried grass, straw and shredded newspaper. These carbon-rich ingredients provide energy for microorganisms to move around in the pile and decompose the materials.

- **1-2 parts Greens (or wet/fresh ingredients).** Examples are fruit and vegetable scraps, coffee grounds, fresh grass clippings, plant clippings, eggshells and tea bags. These nitrogen-rich ingredients provide protein for the microorganisms to survive.

- **Water.** Make sure your compost stays moist so the microorganisms can grow and do their stuff.

- **Air.** Turning the pile helps with decomposition and controls the odors. Who wants a stinky compost heap?

Note: A couple of things to keep out of the pile: meat, dairy products, fats and oils, and human and pet waste.

The Method

As the organic material begins to decompose it will heat up, and you may even see some steam rising from the pile. Use a pitchfork or a shovel to turn your compost pile once a week, once a month or whenever you get around to it. The more you aerate your pile, the faster it will turn into usable compost. If Mother Nature doesn't provide an occasional watering for your pile, you may need to get out the hose and water it yourself.

Even Greener

When your kids have finished their chores, allow them to check out these eco-minded Web sites.

• The Green Squad from the Natural Resources Defense Council (www.nrdc.org/greensquad)

• Kids Recycling Zone (www.kidsrecyclingzone.com)

• Environmental Kids Club from the EPA (www.epa.gov/kids)

• Eekoworld by PBS Kids (www.pbskids.org/eekoworld)

Establish Eco-minded Chores

A lot of eco-minded parents I meet wonder how they can pass their green values to their children. I tell them if they practice what they preach, it will probably sink in—eventually. Meanwhile you can help establish good green habits by giving your kids chores that help build awareness of and appreciation for the environment.

• **Turn off lights.** Set a rule to flip the switch to OFF when rooms around the house are unoccupied.

• **Sort the recycling.** Young children can start with plastics and paper. Older children can sort glass and cans with supervision.

• **Gardening.** Give your child his own little garden plot to tend to. Watering, weeding and harvesting will help him understand that food doesn't just come from the grocery store.

• **Cooking.** Making homemade vegetable soup (with veggies from their garden) as an alternative to canned saves on packaging and tastes much better to boot! Have your children help pick out which vegetables will go in the pot.

• **Volunteer.** Help pick up trash in the neighborhood or do some weeding at the community garden.

Throw a Green Birthday Party

A typical birthday party can be a paper products nightmare, but it doesn't take much to turn it into a greener affair. While you certainly don't want to spoil your child's

200

birthday by not allowing party hats (if that's what is important to her), there are probably some compromises you can make. Think about what works best for you and your child. Make a couple of small changes or turn the party into an all-out eco-extravaganza!

Simple Changes

- Skip paper invites and pick up the phone or use Evites or e-mail instead.

- Choose reusable plates and utensils instead of disposable.

- Serve juice in regular cups instead of buying juice boxes.

- Serve healthy and organic snacks instead of junk food.

- Forgo balloons, party hats and other excessive decorations if you can.

- Skip junky goody bags filled with plastic toys and give thoughtful, practical take-home gifts like art supplies, a book or a small plant.

A Little Bit of Effort

- Bake a homemade birthday cake out of organic ingredients instead of a using boxed mix or buying store-bought cake.

- Make crafts out of recycled materials for a party activity (see *Junk Sculptures* on page 202).

- Create homemade take-home gifts instead of purchasing them. For young children, that could be homemade play dough (see page 76). For older children, a music CD, a small framed photo or a food gift would be nice.

Going All Out

- Have an Earth Day theme and play recycling games or go on a nature treasure hunt.

- Make your own piñata and fill it with organic lollipops, fruit leathers and other healthy snacks.

- Consider an alternative to the traditional party gift:

  - Organize a gift exchange in which everyone brings a gift and goes home with a gift.

  - Suggest that families bring a "previously loved" toy or book instead of buying something new.

  - Consider a gift-free party or recommend a donation to a charity instead of a gift.

Practical Ecocrafts

Here are a few ideas for making useful new items out of materials you would have thrown away. Even someone who doesn't have a crafty bone in their body can handle these super-simple projects.

Junk Sculptures

This can be a fun birthday party activity for older children, but it is also a great rainy day activity to do anytime with minimal preparation. It is a very open-ended project, using whatever materials you have collected from around your house. Supervision is required if you use a hot glue gun, but younger children can use regular glue with terrific results.

What You Need

"Junk" from around the house: paper towel rolls, egg cartons, yogurt cups, tissue boxes, cardboard jewelry boxes, packaging materials, plastic utensils, plastic plant pots—almost anything goes!

Decorations: beads, stones, pipe cleaners, glitter, old game pieces, ribbon scraps, wrapping paper scraps.

Hot glue gun or all-purpose glue

How to Make It

Let your imagination go wild! Make a radio tower, a treasure box, a robot...the possibilities are endless.

DIY Kitchen Scrubbie

You know those mesh plastic bags onions come in? The ones that usually go straight into the trash? Give them a new job as a kitchen scrubbie for pots and pans. Whip one up in no time and get scrubbing!

What You Need

Mesh bag

Rubber band (the wide bands used to bind broccoli stalks together work well)

How to Make It

Step 1: Cut open the mesh bag and lay it flat. Then fold it back and forth accordion-style (like making tissue-paper flowers).

Step 2: Bend the folded mesh in half lengthwise.

Step 3: Twist a rubber band around the fat end.

Plastic Bottle Bubble-ator

Looking for some fun on a hot summer day? This simple craft made from a plastic bottle and an old washcloth will yield loads of bubble fun! This craft idea was originally developed by Betz White. Visit her Web site at www.betzwhite.com.

What You Need

Empty plastic water bottle

Small washcloth or scrap of cotton terry cloth at least 5" x 5" (13cm x 13cm)

Rubber band

Bubble liquid or ecofriendly dish soap

How to Make It

Step 1: Using sharp scissors or a craft knife, cut the bottom off a plastic bottle.

Step 2: Cover the open end with the washcloth or terry cloth and secure with a rubber band.

Step 3: Dip the cloth in water first and then into a plate of bubble liquid or dish soap.

Step 4: Blow forcefully through the top of the bottle. A long tube of bubbles will come pouring out!

Recycled Sweater Bag Dispenser

Getting tired of all the plastic bags cluttering up your cabinets? Look no further than an old sweater for help. The arm of a sweater makes the perfect device for containing those pesky bags, making it easier to grab them when you need them. Simply push the bags through the top of the arm hole and pull them out for use at the wrist end. A ribbon handle at the top makes it easy to hang the dispenser wherever it is convenient.

What You Need

An old wool or wool-blend sweater. It does not need to be machine felted; however, felting will help keep the edges from fraying.

Ribbon

How to Make It

Step 1: Cut the arm off the sweater using a straight cut near the shoulder seam.

Step 2: Snip a hole on each side of the shoulder edge about $3/4"$–$1"$ (19mm–3cm) down from the top.

Step 3: Thread a ribbon through the holes and tie at each side, leaving enough ribbon for a handle at the top.

Step 4: Stuff in your bags, and it's ready to use!

Resources

Further Information
Books:
"Big Green Purse"
by Diane MacEachern

"Green Housekeeping"
by Ellen Sandbeck

"Healthy Child Healthy World"
by Christopher Gavigan

"Naturally Clean"
by Jeffrey Hollender, Geoff Davis and
Meika Hollender

"Not Just a Pretty Face"
by Stacy Malkan

"Raising Baby Green"
by Dr. Alan Greene

"Smart Mama's Green Guide"
by Jennifer Taggart

"Squeaky Green"
by Eric Ryan and Adam Lowry

"The Green Parent"
by Jenn Savedge

"The Virtuous Consumer" by Leslie
Garrett and Peter Greenberg

"What to Eat" by Marion Nestle

Web sites:
Center for Health, Environment & Justice
(www.chej.org)

Children's Environmental Health Network
(www.cehn.org)

Environmental Defense Fund
(www.edf.org)

Environmental Working Group
(www.ewg.org)

Green America
(www.coopamerica.org)

Natural Resources Defense Council
(www.nrdc.org)

Organic Consumers Association
(http://organicconsumers.org)

Organic Trade Association
(http://ota.com)

Women's Voices for the Earth
(www.womenandenvironment.org)

Buying Guides:
Consumer Reports Greener Choices
(www.greenerchoices.org)

Green Guide
(www.thegreenguide.com)

National Green Pages
(www.greenpages.org)

Responsible Shopper
(www.responsibleshopper.org)

CHAPTER 1 – EATING

Co-op Directory Service – An online listing of natural food co-ops (www.coopdirectory.org)

Eat Well Guide – An online directory of family farms and other outlets for locally grown food (www.eatwellguide.org)

Environmental Working Group's FoodNews – Shopper's Guide to Pesticides (www.foodnews.org)

iLunchBox – Healthy recipes and nutritional information for kid-friendly lunches (www.ilunchbox.com)

Local Harvest – Where to find farmers' markets, CSAs and other sources of local food (www.localharvest.org)

Marine Stewardship Council – A certification program and guide to sustainable seafood choices (http://msc.org)

Monterey Bay Aquarium Seafood Watch – A pocket guide and iPhone application for sustainable seafood (www.montereybayaquarium.org/cr/seafoodwatch.aspx)

Sustainable Table – Information about shopping for, cooking and enjoying sustainably raised food (www.sustainabletable.org)

CHAPTER 2 – LIVING

BPA-free Bottles:

Adiri (baby bottles) (www.adiri.com)

BornFree (baby bottles) (www.newbornfree.com)

Klean Kanteen (stainless steel) (http://kleankanteen.com)

Nalgene Everyday (plastic) (http://nalgenechoice.com/everyday.html)

Sigg (lined aluminum) (http://mysigg.com)

silikids (glass bottles) (http://silikids.com)

Wee-go (glass bottles) (www.lifefactory.com)

Food Storage and Lunch Containers:

Kids Konserve (http://kidskonserve.com)

Laptop Lunches (www.laptoplunches.com)

LunchBots (http://lunchbots.com)

ReusableBags (www.reusablebags.com)

Thermos (www.thermos.com)

Wrap-n-Mat (reusable sandwich wrap) (www.wrap-n-mat.com)

Cookware and Bakeware:

GreenPan (available on Amazon.com and at Macy's stores) (http://green-pan.com)

Le Creuset (enameled cast iron) (www.lecreuset.com)

Lodge Cast Iron (http://lodgemfg.com)

Toys:

Bioviva (ecofriendly games) (www.bioviva.com/us)

Craftsbury Kids (toys made in US and Europe; fair trade products) (http://craftsburykids.com)

Green Toys (made in US from 100 percent recycled plastic milk jugs) (http://greentoys.com)

Holgate Toys (classic wooden toys) (www.holgatetoy.com)

Natural Pod (open-ended natural toys) (www.naturalpod.com)

Oompa (natural, wooden and ecofriendly toys) (http://oompa.com)

Peapods (natural toys) (www.peapods.com)

Plan Toys (wooden toys made from natural rubberwood) (http://plantoysusa.com)

Rosie Hippo (wooden toys, games, books and music) (www.rosiehippo.com)

Under the Nile (soft organic toys) (www.underthenile.com)

Craft Supplies:

Aurora Silk (natural fabric dyes) (http://aurorasilk.com)

EcoArtWorks (ecofriendly art supplies) (http://ecoartworks.com)

Makin's Clay (non-PVC clay) (www.makinsclay.com)

Mountain Mist (EcoCraft fiberfill and pillow forms) (http://mountainmistlp.com)

Stubby Pencil Studio (ecofriendly art supplies) (http://stubbypencilstudio.com)

Gadgets:

EnviroGadget (a blog featuring environmentally friendly gadgets) (www.envirogadget.com)

Solio (solar-powered charger) (http://solio.com/charger)

Furniture:

Crate&Barrel (outdoor furniture) (www.crateandbarrel.com)

Gaiam (patio furniture) (www.gaiam.com)

GreenCulture Furniture (ecofriendly furniture) (www.eco-furniture.com)

Play Mart (recycled plastic play equipment) (www.playmart.com)

PolyWood (recycled plastic outdoor furniture) (http://polywoodinc.com)

Smith & Hawken (teak furniture) (www.smithandhawken.com)

Lighting:

GreenCulture Lighting (ecofriendly lighting) (www.eco-lights.com)

Lighting by Gregory (Energy Star light fixtures) (http://lightingbygregory.com)

Mr. Beams (LED lights) (www.mrbeams.com)

Home Office:

GreenLine Paper Company (http://greenlinepaper.com)

TheGreenOffice.com (http://thegreenoffice.com)

Office Depot (www.officedepot.com)

OfficeMax (www.officemax.com)

Staples (www.staples.com)

Zebra Eco (pencils and pens made from recycled materials) (http://zebra-eco.com

Mattresses and Bedding:

Amenity (organic bedding) (www.amenityhome.com)

The Company Store (organic and natural bedding) (www.thecompanystore.com)

Coyuchi (organic bedding) (www.coyuchi.com)

Earthsake (natural and organic bed linens) (http://earthsake.com)

Gaiam (organic cotton bedding and natural pillows) (www.gaiam.com)

Good Night Naturals (organic and natural mattresses and bed linens) (www.goodnightnaturals.com)

The Natural Sleep Store (organic mattresses and bedding): (http://thenaturalsleepstore.com)

Organic Style (high-end organic and natural bedding) (www.organicstyle.com)

Pottery Barn (organic cotton bedding) (www.potterybarn.com)

Rawganique (luxury organic cotton, hemp and linen bedding and pillows) (http://rawganique.com)

Target (affordable organic and natural bed linens) (www.target.com)

West Elm (affordable organic and natural bedding) (www.westelm.com)

CHAPTER 3 - CLEANING
Ecofriendly Cleaning Products:
Biokleen (http://biokleenhome.com)

Bon Ami (www.bonami.com)

Dropps (http://dropps.com)

Earth Friendly Products (www.ecos.com)

Ecostore USA (www.ecostoreusa.com)

Ecover (www.ecover.com)

Green Works (www.greenworkscleaners.com)

Method (www.methodhome.com)

Mountain Green (http://mountaingreen.biz)

Restore (http://restoreproducts.com)

Seventh Generation (www.seventhgeneration.com)

Simple Green (http://simplegreen.com)

Shaklee (www.shaklee.com)

CHAPTER 4 - CARING
Body Care:
Alba (http://albabotanica.com)

Aubrey Organics (www.aubrey-organics.com)

Aura Cacia (www.auracacia.com)

Avalon Organics (http://avalonorganics.com)

Aveda (www.aveda.com)

Burt's Bees (www.burtsbees.com)

Desert Essence (www.desertessence.com)

Dr. Bronner's (www.drbronner.com)

Dr. Hauschka (www.drhauschka.com)

EO (www.eoproducts.com)

evanhealy (www.evanhealy.com)

J.R. Liggett's (www.jrliggett.com)

Kiss My Face (www.kissmyface.com)

Logona (http://logona.com)

Nature's Gate (http://natures-gate.com)

Pangea Organics (www.pangeaorganics.com)

River Soap Company (http://riversoap.com)

suki (www.sukipure.com)

Terressentials (http://terressentials.com)

Tom's of Maine (www.tomsofmaine.com)

Cosmetics, Nail and Hair Care:

Acquarella (www.acquarellapolish.com

Afterglow (http://afterglowcosmetics.com)

Avigal Henna (www.avigalhennausa.com)

Ecco Bella (www.eccobella.com)

EcoColors (www.ecocolors.net)

Gabriel Cosmetics (www.gabrielcosmeticsinc.com)

Giovanni (http://giovannicosmetics.com

Jason (www.jason-natural.com)

Honeybee Gardens (www.honeybeegardens.com)

Miessence (www.miorganicproducts.com)

PeaceKeeper Cause-Metics (www.iama-peacekeeper.com)

Terra Firma (www.terrafirmacosmetics.com)

Infants and Children:

Avalon Organics (baby) (http://avalonorganics.com)

Aveeno Baby (www.aveeno.com/baby)

Burt's Bees (www.burtsbees.com)

California Baby (www.californiababy.com)

Earth Mama Angel Baby (www.earthmamaangelbaby.com)

Kiss My Face Kids (www.kissmyface.com)

Little Earth's Beauty Children Makeup (www.allnaturalcosmetics.com)

Nature's Baby Organics (www.natures-babyproducts.com)

Piggy Paint (www.piggypaint.com)

Teens Turning Green (line at Whole Foods) (www.teensturninggreen.org)

TruKid (http://trukid.com)

Weleda (www.weleda.com)

Diapers:

DiaperSwappers (www.diaperswappers.com)

gDiapers (www.gdiapers.com)

Seventh Generation (www.seventhgeneration.com/diapers)

Tushies (www.tushies.com)

Homemade Body Care Ingredients and Packaging:

Aromaland (www.aromaland.com)

Cranberry Lane (http://cranberrylane.stores.yahoo.net)

Mountain Rose Herbs (http://mountain-roseherbs.com)

SunFeather (http://sunfeather.com)

210

CHAPTER 5 - CLOTHING

Retail Stores:

American Apparel (www.americanapparel.com)

Gap (www.gap.com)

H&M (www.hm.com)

Levi Strauss & Co. (www.levistrauss.com)

Patagonia (www.patagonia.com)

REI (www.rei.com)

Online Resources:

Bamboosa (www.bamboosa.com)

Birch (http://birchclothing.com)

Gaiam (www.gaiam.com)

Garnet Hill (www.garnethill.com)

Greenloop (www.thegreenloop.com)

LotusOrganics.com (http://lotusorganics.com)

Rawganique (http://rawganique.com)

Brands of Note:

Blue Canoe (www.bluecanoe.com)

Certified Jeans (http://certifiedjean.com

CottonfieldUSA (www.cottonfieldusa.com)

Del Forte (http://delforte.com)

Earth (www.earthfootwear.com)

Ecolution (www.ecolution.com)

Edun (http://edunonline.com)

Eileen Fisher (http://eileenfisher.com)

Icebreaker (www.icebreaker.com)

Loomstate Organic (http://loomstate.org)

Loyale (http://loyaleclothing.com)

Naturally Bamboo (http://naturallybambooclothing.com)

Stewart + Brown (http://stewartbrown.com)

Timberland (www.timberland.com)

Tinctoria (http://tinctoriadesigns.com)

Truly Organic (http://truly-organic.com)

Simple Shoes (www.simpleshoes.com)

Maggie's Organics (http://maggiesorganics.com)

Infants and Children:

B nature (http://bnatureorganic.com)

Babysoy (www.babysoyusa.com)

Hanna Andersson (www.hannaandersson.com)

Kate Quinn Organics (www.katequinnorganics.com)

KidBean.com (www.kidbean.com)

The Little Seed (http://thelittleseed.com)

Obli Organics (www.obliorganics.com)

Sage Creek Organics (http://sagecreekorganics.com)

Puddlegear (http://puddlegear.com)

speesees (http://speesees.com)

Fair Trade:

Fair Indigo (www.fairindigo.com)

Global Girlfriend (http://globalgirlfriend.com)

Global Mamas (http://globalmamas.org)

Indigenous (http://indigenousdesigns.com)

Justice Clothing (www.justiceclothing.com)

Marigold Fair Trade Clothing (www.marigoldfairtradeclothing.com)

No Sweat (http://nosweatapparel.com)

Original Good (www.originalgood.com)

Ten Thousand Villages (www.tenthousandvillages.com)

Thrift and Resale Stores:

Buffalo Exchange
(http://buffaloexchange.com)

Crossroads Trading Co.
(http://crossroadstrading.com

Goodwill Industries (www.goodwill.org)

Once Upon a Child (www.ouac.com)

Plato's Closet (teen fashion) (http://plato-scloset.com)

Play It Again Sports (sports clothing and equipment)
(http://playitagainsports.com)

Ragstock (midwest) (www.ragstock.com)

The Salvation Army
(http://salvationarmyusa.org)

Fabric and Yarn:

Aurora Silk (fabric, yarn and natural fabric dyes) (http://aurorasilk.com)

Harmony Art (fabric)
(http://harmonyart.com)

Hemp Traders (hemp fabric) (http://hemptraders.com)

Lanaknits Designs (hemp for knitting)
(www.lanaknits.com)

Lion Brand Yarn (http://lionbrand.com)

Llamajama (wool yarn)
www.llamajama.com

Mimi the Sardine (PVC-free waterproof fabric) (www.mimithesardine.com)

Mod Green Pod (organic cotton canvas)
(http://modgreenpod.com)

NearSea Naturals (natural and organic fabrics)
(www.nearseanaturals.com)

Organic Cotton Plus (organic cotton fabrics) (http://organiccottonplus.com)

PM Organics (organic cotton fabrics)
(http://pmorganics.com)

CHAPTER 6 – CONSERVING

Recycling Resources:

The Container Store
(www.containerstore.com)

Earth911 (www.earth911.com)

National Recycling Coalition (www.nrc-recycle.org)

Storables (www.storables.com)

Composting Resources:

US Environmental Protection Agency
(www.epa.gov/epawaste/conserve/rrr/composting)

Gardener's Supply (www.gardeners.com/composters)

Howtocompost.org (www.howtocompost.org)

Green Birthday Party Supplies:

Green Party Goods (www.greenparty-goods.com)

Kids Konserve www.kidskonserve.com

Preserve www.recycline.com

Notes

CHAPTER 1 – EATING

"Labeling Packaged Products." Agricultural Marketing Service. U.S. Department of Agriculture, National Organic Program. 9 Jan. 2003 <http://www.ams.usda.gov/AMSv1.0/getfile?dDocName=STELDEV3004323&acct=nopgeninfo>.

Benbrook, Charles, Xin Zhao, Jaime Yañez, Neal Davies and Preston Andrews. "New Evidence Confirms the Nutritional Superiority of Plant-Based Organic Foods." State of Science Review. The Organic Center. March 2008 <http://www.organic-center.org/science.nutri.php?action=view&report_id=126>.

"Shopper's Guide to Pesticides." Environmental Working Group. March 2009 <http://www.foodnews.org/walletguide.php>.

"Are Organic Foods as Good as They're Grown?" Consumer Reports. ConsumersUnion.org. 15 Dec. 1997 <http://www.consumersunion.org/pub/core_food_safety/002316.html>.

Baker, Brian P., Charles M. Benbrook, Edward Groth III and Karen Lutz Benbrook. "Pesticide Residues in Conventional, IPM-Grown and Organic Foods: Insights from Three US Data Sets." Food Additives and Contaminants 19:5 (May 2002) <http://www.consumersunion.org/food/organicsumm.htm>.

Minowa, Craig. "U.S. Government Facts: Children's Chemical & Pesticide Exposure via Food Products." Organic Consumers Association. July 2005 <http://www.organicconsumers.org/organic/wic-faq.pdf>.

Jacobson, Michael F. "Pumped-Up Poultry Not 'Natural'" Center for Science in the Public Interest. 22 May 2007 <http://www.cspinet.org/nah/vlog/poultry.html>.

Glazer, Sarah. "Slow Food Movement." CQ Researcher 73-96.

Koch, Kathy. "Food Safety Battle: Organic vs. Biotech." CQ Researcher 4 Sept. 1998: 761-784.

Weeks, Jennifer. "Factory Farms." CQ Researcher 12 Jan. 2007: 25-48.

Weeks, Jennifer. "Buying Green." CQ Researcher 2 Feb. 2008: 193-216.

"The Dirty Dozen." Prevention Magazine. 2 Oct. 2006 <http://www.prevention.com/cda/article/the-dirty-dozen/a323b0b803110VgnVCM20000012281eac___/nutrition.recipes/grocery.guru/food.safety.basics>.

Greene, Dr. Alan. "Dr. Greene's Organic Prescription." Dr. Greene. 20 March 2009 <http://www.drgreene.com/555560.html>.

McKay, Betsy. "When Buying Organic Makes Sense and When it Doesn't." Wall Street Journal. 16 Jan 2007 <http://online.

wsj.com/article/SB116891484181777282.
html>.

"Benefits of Organic." Organic Trade
Association. 2008 <http://www.ota.com/
organic/benefits.html>.

"Top Scientists Urge Food Standards
Agency to Recognize Nutritional
Difference of Organic Milk." The Organic
Milk Cooperative. 29 Aug. 2006
<http://www.omsco.co.uk/index.cfm/
organicmilk/Media.PressRelease/release-
id/53/subject>.

Epstein, Samuel S., M.D. "What's in Your
Milk?" Organic Consumer's Association.
2006 <http://www.organicconsumers.
org/rbghlink.cfm>.

"Seven Reasons Why Kids Should Drink
Organic Milk." Organic Valley Family of
Farms. 23 May 2005 <http://www.organ-
icvalley.coop/resources/health-nutrition-
links>.

Leu, Andre. "The Benefits of Organic
Food." Organic Valley Family of Farms
2009 < http://www.organicvalley.coop/
resources/reading-room/benefits>.

Motavalli, Jim. "The Meat of the Matter."
E Magazine 19:4 (July/August 2008).

"The Promise and Perils of Fish Farming."
Environmental Defense Fund. 30
Oct. 2007 <http://www.edf.org/page.
cfm?tagID=16150>.

"What You Need to Know about Mercury
in Fish and Shellfish." Environmental
Protection Agency. 18 Nov. 2008 <http://
www.epa.gov/waterscience/fish/advice>.

"Seafood Watch." Monterey Bay
Aquarium. 2009 <http://www.monterey-
bayaquarium.org/cr/SeafoodWatch/web/
sfw_factsheet.aspx>.

"Bisphenol A: Toxic Plastics Chemical
in Canned Food: Canned Food Test
Results." Environmental Working Group.
5 March 2007 <http://www.ewg.org/
node/20933>.

CHAPTER 2 - LIVING

"Smart Plastics Guide." Institute for Agriculture and Trade Policy. Oct. 2005 <http://www.agobservatory.org/library.cfm?refid=77083>.

Shelton, Deborah. "Study: BPA Linked to Heart Disease, Diabetes, Liver Problems." Chicago Tribune. 16 Sept. 2008 <http://www.ewg.org/node/27138>.

"Lead in Lunch Boxes FAQs." Center for Environmental Health. 2008 <http://www.ceh.org/index.php?option=com_content&task=view&id=169&Itemid=178>.

"Perfluorooctanoic Acid (PFOA) and Fluorinated Telomers" Environmental Protection Agency. 19 March 2009 <http://www.epa.gov/opptintr/pfoa/index.htm>.

Hoffman, Mathew, M.D. "Pots, Pans, and Plastics: A Shopper's Guide to Food Safety." WebMD. 6 March 2009 <http://www.ewg.org/node/27686>.

"Chemical Families: Lead Compounds." Environmental Working Group. 2009 <http://www.ewg.org/chemindex/term/455>.

"BodyBurden: Phthalates." Environmental Working Group. 2009 <http://www.ewg.org/featured/227>.

"The Poison Plastic." Greenpeace International. 2009 <http://www.greenpeace.org/international/campaigns/toxics/polyvinyl-chloride/the-poison-plastic>.

Miller, Jordana. "Tests Reveal High Chemical Levels in Kids' Bodies." CNN. 22 Oct. 2007 <http://www.cnn.com/2007/TECH/science/10/22/body.burden/index.html>.

"Q&A on the Environmental Benefits of Recycled Paper." Environmental Defense. 2009 <http://www.coopamerica.org/PDF/QandAPaper.pdf>.

"Paper Production and Consumption Facts." Green America. 2009 <http://www.coopamerica.org/programs/woodwise/consumers/stats/index.cfm>.

"Polybrominated diphenylethers (PBDEs)." Environmental Protection Agency. 23 Dec. 2008 <http://www.epa.gov/oppt/pbde>.

CHAPTER 3 - CLEANING

"The Inside Story: A Guide to Indoor Air Quality." Environmental Protection Agency. 26 Jan. 2009 <http://www.epa.gov/iaq/pubs/insidest.html>.

Gorman, Alexandra. "Household Hazards: Potential Hazards of Home Cleaning Products." Women's Voices for the Earth. July 2007 <http://www.womenandenvironment.org/campaignsandprograms/SafeCleaning/HazardsReport.pdf>.

"Asthma and Household Cleaning Products." Women's Voices for the Earth. 2009 <http://www.womenandenvironment.org/campaignsandprograms/SafeCleaning/asthma>.

"Many Cleaners, Air Fresheners May Pose Health Risks When Used Indoors." Science Daily. 24 May 2006 <http://www.sciencedaily.com/releases/2006/05/060524123900.htm>.

"Hidden Hazards in Air Fresheners." Natural Resources Defense Council 20 Sept. 2007 <http://www.nrdc.org/health/home/airfresheners/contents.asp>.

"Reducing Worker Exposure to Perchloroethylene (PERC) in Dry Cleaning." United States Department of Labor, Occupational Safety and Health Administration. 12 April 2005 <http://www.osha.gov/dsg/guidance/perc.html>.

"An Introduction to Indoor Air Quality." Environmental Protection Agency. 26 Jan. 2009 <http://www.epa.gov/iaq/voc.html>.

"Greening Your Purchase of Cleaning Products: A Guide For Federal Purchasers." Environmental Protection Agency. 7 Nov. 2007 <http://www.epa.gov/epp/pubs/cleaning.htm>.

"Pesticide in Soap, Toothpaste and Breast Milk - Is It Kid-Safe?: EWG's Guide to Triclosan." Environmental Working Group. 2009. <http://www.ewg.org/node/26721>.

"The Chlorine Conundrum." The Green Guide. 1 March 2003 <http://www.thegreenguide.com/greenguide/home-garden/cleaning/chlorine-conundrum/2>.

"Diethanolamine and Cosmetic Products." US Food and Drug Administration. 27 Oct. 2006. <http://www.cfsan.fda.gov/~dms/cos-dea.html>.

"Chlorine." Environmental Protection Agency. Jan. 2000 <http://www.epa.gov/ttn/atw/hlthef/chlorine.html>.

Cohen, Alison, Sarah Janssen and Gina Solomon. "Clearing the Air: Hidden Hazards of Air Fresheners." Natural Resources Defense Council. Sept. 2007 <http://www.nrdc.org/health/home/airfresheners/airfresheners.pdf>.

Fischer, Douglas. "The Body Chemical." Oakland Tribune. 15 March 2005 <http://www.ewg.org/node/17256>.

"Third National Report on Human Exposure to Environmental Chemicals." Center for Disease Control and Prevention. 2005 <http://www.cdc.gov/exposurereport>.

CHAPTER 4 - CARING

"OCA & Dr. Bronner's Challenge Weak Ecocert & OASIS Standards." Organic Consumers Association. 17 March 2008 <http://www.organicconsumers.org/bodycare/OASISrelease080317.cfm>.

Stay, Flora D.D.S. "Are You Giving Your Child a Daily Dose of Toxins?" Natural News. 28 Aug. 2008 <http://www.naturalnews.com/z024013.html>.

Hopkins, Virginia. "Why Scented Products (Fakegrances) Are Not Safe." Natural News. 11 Aug. 2008 <http://www.naturalnews.com/z023830.html>.

"Pesticides in the Diets of Infants and Children." The National Academies Press. 1993 <http://www.nap.edu/openbook.php?record_id=2126&page=1>.

Houlihan, Jane, Charlotte Brody and Bryony Schwan. "Not Too Pretty: Phthalates, Beauty Products and the FDA." Environmental Working Group. 8 July 2002 <http://safecosmetics.org/downloads/NotTooPretty_report.pdf>

Sutton, Rebecca PhD. "Adolescent Exposures to Cosmetic Chemicals of Concern." Environmental Working Group. Sept. 2008 <http://www.ewg.org/reports/teens>.

Howard, Brian. "Cosmetic Labeling." The Green Guide. 2009 <http://www.thegreenguide.com/personal-care/cosmetic-labeling>.

Epstein, Samuel S. "Opinion: Beware Carcinogens, Phthalates in Cosmetics."

Environment News Service. 14 July 2002 <http://www.ewg.org/node/14943>.

"Chemical Families: Phthalates." Environmental Working Group. 2009 <http://www.ewg.org/chemindex/term/480>

"Cosmetics, Body Care Products, and Personal Care Products." Agricultural Marketing Service. April 2008 <http://www.ams.usda.gov/AMSv1.0/getfile?dDocName=STELPRDC5068442>.

"Body Burden—The Pollution in Newborns." Environmental Working Group. 14 July 2005 <http://archive.ewg.org/reports/bodyburden2/execsumm.php>.

"Skin Deep—Report on Cosmetics & Skincare." Choose Organics. <http://www.chooseorganics.com/organicarticles/skin_deep_report.htm>.

"Why This Matters." Environmental Working Group. 2009 <http://www.cosmeticsdatabase.com/research/whythismatters.php>.

"Teen Girls' Body Burden of Hormone-Altering Cosmetics Chemicals: Detailed Findings." Environmental Working Group. 2009 <http://www.ewg.org/node/26954>.

"Carcinogenic 1,4-dioxane Found in Leading 'Organic' Brand Personal Care Products." Organic Consumers Association. 14 March 2008 <http://www.organicconsumers.org/bodycare/DioxaneRelease08.cfm>.

"A Shopper's Guide to Home Tissue Products." Natural Resources Defense Council. 26 Oct. 2005 <http://www.nrdc.org/land/forests/gtissue.asp#toilet>.

CHAPTER 5 - CLOTHING

"Co-op America's Guide to Ending Sweatshops." Co-op America. 2008 <http://www.coopamerica.org/PDF/EndingSweatshops.pdf>.

"The Deadly Chemicals in Cotton." Environmental Justice Foundation. 2007 <http://www.ejfoundation.org/pdf/the_deadly_chemicals_in_cotton.pdf>.

Gorman, James. "Frankencotton, the Shirt: Coming Soon to a Wardrobe Near You." The New York Times. 16 May 2006 <http://www.nytimes.com/2006/05/16/science/16side.html?ex=1305432000&en=b9949335e1113f6d&ei=5090&partner=rssuserland&emc=rss>.

"Genetically Modified Cotton: Manufacturers May Soon Be Reaping What They Sow." Sustainable Cotton Project. 2009 <http://www.sustainable-cotton.org/html/consumers/GM_cotton.html>.

Claudio, Luz. "Waste Couture: Environmental Impact of the Clothing Industry." Environmental Health Perspectives 115:9 (Sept. 2007). <http://www.ehponline.org/members/2007/115-9/focus.html>.

"Organic Cotton Facts." Organic Trade Association. Feb. 2009 <http://www.ota.com/organic/mt/organic_cotton.html>.

Sherman, Cathy. "Do You Know What Toxic Chemicals Lurk in Your Clothing?" Natural News. 10 March 2008 <http://www.naturalnews.com/z022803.html>.

"Synthetic Dyes: A Look at Environmental & Human Risks." Green Cotton. 18 June 2008 <http://greencotton.wordpress.com/2008/06/18/synthetic-dyes-a-look-at-the-good-the-bad-and-the-ugly>.

"Organic Cotton Output Soars." EcoTextile News. 10 Sept. 2008 <http://www.ecotextile.com/news_details.php?id=873>.

"Organic Cotton Market Report: Preliminary Highlights." Organic Exchange. 2007 <http://www.organic-exchange.org/Documents/market_high_fall07.pdf>.

"Bamboo Sprouting Green Myths." Organic Clothing. 1 Aug. 2008 <http://organicclothing.blogs.com/my_weblog/2008/08/bamboo-sprouting-green-myths.html>.

CHAPTER 6 - CONSERVING

"EPA—Municipal Solid Waste Generation, Recycling, and Disposal in the United States: Facts and Figures for 2006." US Environmental Protection Agency. Nov. 2007 <http://www.epa.gov/epawaste/non-haz/municipal/pubs/msw06.pdf>.

"Municipal Solid Waste in the United States: Facts and Figures for 2007." US Environmental Protection Agency. Nov. 2008 <http://www.epa.gov/epawaste/nonhaz/municipal/pubs/msw07-rpt.pdf>.

Oliver, Rachel. "All About: Food Waste." CNN. 22 Jan. 2008 <http://www.cnn.com/2007/WORLD/asiapcf/09/24/food.leftovers/index.html#cnnSTCText>.

"Water Usage." Washington Suburban Sanitary Commission. 2009 <http://www.wssc.dst.md.us/service/waterusagechart.cfm>.

"Water Use Statistics." American Waterworks Association. 2009 <http://www.drinktap.org/consumerdnn/Default.aspx?tabid=85>.

"25 Simple Ways to Save." Consumer Reports Oct. 2008 <http://www.consumerreports.org/cro/home-garden/resource-center/saving-on-energy-costs/25-simple-ways-to-save/saving-on-energy-costs-simple-ways-to-save.htm?resultPageIndex=1&resultIndex=1&searchTerm=ways%20to%20save%20water>.

"Recycling Facts." Oberlin College. 2008 <http://www.oberlin.edu/recycle/facts.html>.

"Recycling Benefits: The Many Reasons Why." Recycling Revolution. 2009 <http://www.recycling-revolution.com/recycling-benefits.html>.

"How Recycling Can Help Stop Global Warming." Help Stop Global Warming. 2007 <http://www.help-stop-global-warming.com/global-warming-recycling.html>.

"A Consumer's Guide to Energy Efficiency and Renewable Energy." US Department of Energy. 23 March 2009 <http://apps1.eere.energy.gov/consumer>.

"One-Quarter of Americans Do Not Recycle in Their Own Home." The Harris Poll 67. 11 July 2007 <http://www.harrisinteractive.com/harris_poll/index.asp?PID=783>. Crayon Cupcakes, 77

Index